# The
# Year
## of the
# Poet VII

## December 2020

**The Poetry Posse**

*inner child press, ltd.*

# The Poetry Posse 2020

Gail Weston Shazor

Shareef Abdur Rasheed

Teresa E. Gallion

hülya n. yılmaz

Kimberly Burnham

Tzemin Ition Tsai

Elizabeth Esguerra Castillo

Jackie Davis Allen

Joe Paire

Caroline 'Ceri' Nazareno

Ashok K. Bhargava

Alicja Maria Kuberska

Swapna Behera

Albert 'Infinite' Carrasco

Eliza Segiet

William S. Peters, Sr.

~ * ~

In order to maintain each poet's authentic voice, this volume has not undergone the scrutiny of editing. Please take time to indulge each contributor for their own creativity and aspirations to convey their uniqueness.

hülya n. yılmaz, Ph.D.
Director of Editing ~
Inner Child Press International

# General Information

## The Year of the Poet VII
### December 2020 Edition

## The Poetry Posse

### 1st Edition : 2020

### Publisher Information
#### 1st Edition : Inner Child Press
intouch@innerchildpress.com
www.innerchildpress.com

ISBN-13 : 978-1-952081-36-1 (inner child press, ltd.)

$ 12.99

# WHAT WOULD LIFE BE WITHOUT A LITTLE POETRY?

# Dedication

This Book is dedicated to

## Humanity, Peace & Poetry

the Power of the Pen

can effectuate change!

&

## The Poetry Posse

past, present & future

our Patrons and Readers

the Spirit of our Everlasting Muse

*In the darkness of my life*
*I heard the music*
*I danced . . .*
*and the Light appeared*
*and I dance*

Janet P. Caldwell

# Table of Contents

# The Poetry Posse

# Table of Contents . . . *continued*

# December's Featured Poets     113

# Inner Child News     151

# Other Anthological Works     179

# Foreword

The present volume marks the end of a year – the pandemic-stricken 2020. COVID-19 is out in full force in numerous countries, with the U.S. having the highest active cases and fatalities. Diverse data suggest that some countries have either not reported anything specific regarding the virus or their population has not been affected. Turkmenistan and North Korea are two instances where related reports are suspected to have been suppressed; hence, displaying zero incidences. There are, however, island nations in the South Pacific – Palau, Micronesia, Kiribati, Tuvalu, Samoa and Tonga, which seemed to have been spared by the virus' spread due to their isolated locations. Still, Vanuatu, Fiji and Solomon have been under its impact.

While the Damocles' sword continues to swing this year over the majority of nations – disguised not only as a highly contagious virus but also in various forms of persistent political turbulences, thoughts of enduring peace worldwide have maintained their place in countless hearts. 2020's final issue of *The Year of the Poet* is its own evidence. Writers from across the globe have once more come together as a collective voice through the uniting power of poetry to contemplate on peace for humanity. The poems in this collection speak for themselves. As for this month's focal defender of peace, the 2019 Nobel

Peace Prize recipient Abiy Ahmed Ali, a considerable amount of information is being provided through the poetic constructs but also as introductory prose. There remains one point that needs to be emphatically stated: even the mere conceptualization of peace for the sake of an oppressed populace is of vital importance. Abiy Ahmed Ali's dedication to the actual application of that concept and his ensuing initiatives against his country's oppressive regime have, after all, materialized as peace not only in his native land, Ethiopia, but also in the neighboring Eritrea.

Albert Einstein has been quoted as having said the following: "Peace cannot be kept by force. It can only be achieved by understanding." Together with Abiy Ahmed Ali and innumerable other defenders of peace – recognized worldwide or not, we thus join hands yet once again toward a comprehensive understanding for the only alternative that there is when the survival and betterment of humanity in its entirety is concerned: a growing platform of peaceful coexistence where oppressive powers that be are not allowed any place or space.

hülya n. yılmaz, Ph.D.

Professor Emerita, The Pennsylvania State University (U.S.A.)
Director of Editing Services, Inner Child Press International (U.S.A.)

# Preface

Dear Family and Friends,

Yes I am excited and feel accomplished as we are now piublishing the final volume (#84) of our seventh year. This most definitely has been a worthy enterprise, *The Year of the Poet*.

This year we have aligned our vision with that of Nober Peace Prize Recipients. We have title this year's theme. The Year of Peace! Hopefully thorugh our sharing each month, our poetry can have a profound effect on our global consciousness and the need for peace while educating ourselves and our readership about some of the individuals who have made history through their efforts to promulgate peace for all of humanity.. We are on our way to hitting yet another milestone. Needless to say, I am elated.

To reiterate, our initial vision was to just perform at this level for the year of 2014. Since that time we have had the blessed opportunity to include many other wonderful poets, word artists and storytellers in the Poetry Posse from lands, cultures and persuasions all over the world. We have featured hundreds of additional poets, thereby introducing their poetic offerings to our vast global audience.

In keeping with our effort and vision to expand the awareness of poets from all walks by making this offerings accessible, we at Inner Child Press International will continue to make every volume a FREE Download. The books are also available for purchase at the affordable cost of $7.00 per volume.

In the previous years, our monthly themes were Flowers, Birds, Gemstones, Trees and Past Cultures. This coming year we have elected to continue our focus of choosing what we consider a significant subject . . . PEACE! In each month's volume you will have the opportunity to not only read at least one poem themed by our Poetry Posse members about such celebrated Peace Ambassadors, but we have included a few words about each individual in our prologue. We hope you find the poetic offerings insightful as we use our poetic form to relay to you what we too have learned through our research in making our offering available to you, our readership.

In closing, we would like to thank you for being an integral part of our amazing journey.

Enjoy our amazing featured poets . . . they are amazing!

*Building Cultural Bridges of Understanding . . .*

Bless Up . . . From the home in our hearts to yours


*Bill*

The Poetry Posse
Inner Child Press Ineternational


PS

Do Not forget about the World Healing, World
Peace Poetry effort.

Available here

www.worldhealingworldpeacepoetry.com

**For Free Downloads of Previous Issues of
The Year of the Poet**

www.innerchildpress.com/the-year-of-the-poet

# World Healing World Peace
## 2020

Poets for Humanity

*Now Available*

www.innerchildpress.com/world-healing-
world-peace-poetry

www.worldhealingworldpeacepoetry.com

www.worldhealingworldpeacefoundation.org

# Abiy Ahmed Ali
## 2019

Each month for the year of 2020, which we have deemed as *The Year of Peace*, we at Inner Child Press International will be celebrating through our poetry a few Nobel Peace Prize Recipients who have contributed greatly to humanity via their particular avocations. This month of Julu 2020 you will find select poems from each Poetry Posse member on this month's celebrants.

In 2019, The Nobel Peace Prize was awarded to Abiy Ahmed Ali

### For more information about visit :

www.nobelprize.org/prizes/peace/2019/abiy/facts

https://en.wikipedia.org/wiki/Abiy_Ahmed

World Healing, World Peace Foundation
*human beings for humanity*

worldhealingworldpeacefoundation.org

Poets . . .
sowing seeds in the
Conscious Garden of Life,
that those who have yet to come
may enjoy the Flowers.

Poets, Writers . . . know that we are the enchanting magicians that nourishes the seeds of dreams and thoughts . . . it is our words that entice the hearts and minds of others to believe there is something grand about the possibilities that life has to offer and our words tease it forth into action . . . for you are the Poet, the Writer to whom the Gift of Words has been entrusted . . .

~ wsp

*poetry is . . .*

Poetry succeeds where instruction fails.

~ wsp

i FLY

because

... said the Dreamer to the world.

I Can

www.iamjustbrill.com

# Gail Weston Shazor

This is a creative promise ~ my pen will speak to and for the world. Enamored with letters and respectful of their power, I have been writing for most of my life. A mother, daughter, sister and grandmother I give what I have been given, greatfilledly.

Author of . . .

"An Overstanding of an Imperfect Love"
&
Notes from the Blue Roof

Lies My Grandfathers Told Me

available at Inner Child Press.

www.facebook.com/gailwestonshazor
www.innerchildpress.com/gail-weston-shazor
navypoet1@gmail.com

# Gail Weston Shazor

*"They have not seen the fear,*
*They have not seen the fatigue,*
*They have not seen the destruction or heartbreak,*
*Nor have they felt the mournful emptiness of war after the*
*carnage."*
*~Abiy Ahmed Ali*

*(Nonet)*

We
Often
Overthink
What we would do
When faced with danger
In the heat of moments
But the real truth remains this
We will only seek to survive
The war we often find ourselves in
When men nor talk or listen to others

# Blue Roof 1945

I cannot sleep.
I walk to and fro
Oblivious to the dampness
That set the bones
To shudder
And I say out loud
Thy will be done and
All the other pithies
That will set me
In Your perfect will
But
I am not
In agreement with You
I mutter curses
With the very breath
That You have given me
For I cannot fathom
The world that You
Have allowed me
To have the barest glimpse of
This boneless world
This broken world
That would steal the very tears
From my reluctant sight
And I rail
Against the cleaved in two
Thing that You ask of me
I am not strong enough
To anchor myself
So why must this
Be my mantle?
And You set this Mary task
At my Martha feet
The same steps that should
Shroud my days

As familiars, I reject
Again and again
I clutch my breast
As each knell falls hollow
And I
With my child choice
Would not deliberately
Pick the pain
Although I long for blue splinters
So that I know
I am still alive
On this mortal plane
And the heart of the tinman
That has muttered
Since You blew into this clay
Beats an irregular rhythm
Give me the easy words
To live through
The coming tribulation
Let the love that quickens
Shine through
All the broken places
For only You know
Just how many there really are
Ease my pace
So that I can be caught
And held
Among the steps
Under my feet
To accept the comforter
That You send
Sweeten my tongue
So that muteness
Is not my lot.
And rest my body
So my soul will heal

# Death in a Foreign Land

There was nothing exciting about it. The day started out much as the day before had, with the sun rising hot before one was ready to leave the house. The roosters crowed their regular untimely noise loud enough to wake the dead.

Life calls loudly
In the midday sun
Anybody with anybody's
Time under this hot sky
Knew the sound by heart
The keening wail broke the stride
Of those by passers
Quickening steps less they find
That their numbers had been chosen also
Death was upon the land
It elevated the cries to a pitch

She was just an ordinary girl and everyone knew her even if they didn't know her name. She was well seen hustling along the docks. One day selling flowers, the next teas and when she couldn't steal something sellable, herself had to do.

The smile below her mouth
Shines a bright red
In the morning light
No one could mistake the double grin
For happiness
This look had circled the world
Surprise at the suddenness
Of the end of life

The policeman showed up after receiving the call. His impotence at preventing the violence wrought upon the public daily showing in the sweat on his brow. There was nothing he

could do for her now but go through the motions of asking
questions of the people around.

What more could he know
Save the dead girl's name
Her real name gifted her at birth
The only real thing she owned
And the one thing she had protected
From being stolen from her
Unspoken and not be heard again
Passing her birth mouth
And not the one gifted at her death

She lay half in the water and half out. No one knew how long
she had been there, but it was obvious it had been

a while. He estimated from the lack of rigidity that she had
lain here most of the night. He knew before he took

out his notebook, that no one had seen anything nor heard
anything. With a sigh, he removed a pencil from his pocket.

The business end lay on the stone
The accidental end, in the water
The very thing that hastened her death
Had begun to melt in the surf
Her last bit of currency
Returning to the source until
Only androgyny remained under the sun.

# Alicja Maria Kuberska

Alicja Maria Kuberska – awarded Polish poetess, novelist, journalist, editor.

She is a member of the Polish Writers Associations in Warsaw, Poland and IWA Bogdani, Albania. She is also a member of directors' board of Soflay Literature Foundation, Our Poetry Archive (India) and Cultural Ambassador for Poland (Inner Child Press, USA )

Her poems have been published in numerous anthologies and magazines in : Poland, Czech Republic, Slovakia, Hungary,Ukraina, Belgium, Bulgaria, Albania, Spain, the UK, Italy, the USA, Canada, the UK, Argentina, Chile, Peru, Israel, Turkey, India, Uzbekistan, South Korea, Taiwan, China, Australia, South Africa, Zambia, Nigeria

She received two medals - the Nosside UNESCO Competition in Italy (2015) and European Academy of Science Arts and Letters in France (2017). Ahe also received a reward of international literary competition in Italy „ Tra le parole e 'elfinito" (2018). She was announced a poet of the 2017 year by Soflay Literature Foundation (2018).She also received : Bolesław Prus Prize Poland (2019), Culture Animator Poland (2019) and first prize Premio Internazionale di Poesia Poseidonia- Paestrum Italy (2019).

# Let's Tear Down Walls, Let's Build Bridges!
*(Dedicated To Abiy Ahmed Ali)*

The new road is blocked by the old wall,
built out of prejudice, feud and intolerance.
It has to be demolished in order to continue.
It's necessary to overcome further obstacles
and throw the bridge across the river
to meet people on its other side.

One should follow the voice of wisdom.
You mustn't give up and
believe in the words of the skeptics,
that one man cannot change the world.
Step by step, word for word,
today is taking shape

To be a philosopher and a Prime Minister,
to be a Muslim and a Christian,
to be a soldier and strive for peace
— Just believe in yourself.

## Autumn melancholy

Melancholy returned home in November
and she started to  live in all the rooms
She placed dim light in the windows
and scattered the seeds of sorrow on the threshold

In the evenings, she summons ghosts and memories
Her relatives  resurrect from old photos
and they tell forgotten stories and anecdotes
Their lives take again timid blushes


Look - she announces to all her friends
Laughing pumpkins and cascades of rustling candies
do not match my interior decorations  at all.
I don't open my door to the bunches of impish kids

## All Saints Day

The night frost stripped the cemetery trees.
The colorful, damp rug rustles underfoot.
It rises and falls, the soft murmur of falling leaves
says prayers for all who are absent.

The flames of the candles flicker and sway in the wind,
illuminating  the barely visible path to heaven
Today you can only meet  halfway
 in  your memories and in rosary beads.

The good –looking chrysanthemums are love confessions
Instead of words, they use the colors and the fragility of
    petals
They decorate granite slabs and graves with crosses,
on which,  time slowly blurs the traces of memory.

A marble angel is sitting and crying on a small grave.
The morning dew hung tears on his stone  eyes.
He is silent and sadness flashes in big drops.
The angel is filled with remorse, he did not guard.

Jackie
Davis
Allen

Jackie Davis Allen

Jackie Davis Allen, otherwise known as Jacqueline D. Allen or Jackie Allen, grew up in the Cumberland Mountains of Appalachia.  As the next eldest daughter of a coal miner father and a stay at home mother, she was the first in her family to attend and graduate from college.  Her siblings, in their own right, are accomplished, though she is the only one, to date, that has discovered the gift of writing.

Graduating from Radford University, with a Bachelors of Science degree in Early Education, she taught in both public and private schools.  For over a decade she taught private art classes to children both in her home and at a local Art and Framing Shop where she also sold her original soft sculptured Victorian dolls and original christening gowns.

She resides in northern Virginia with her husband, taking much needed get-aways to their mountain home near the Blue Ridge Mountains, a place that evokes memories of days spent growing up in the Appalachian Mountains.

A lover of hats, she has worn many.  Following marriage to her college sweetheart, and as wife, mother, grandmother, teacher, tutor, artist, writer, poet and crafter, she is a lover of art and antiques, surrounding herself, always, with books, seeking to learn more.

In 2015 she authored *Looking for Rainbows, Poetry, Prose and Art*, and in 2017, *Dark Side of the Moon*.  Both books of mostly narrative poetry were published by Inner Child Press and were edited by hulya n. yilmaz.

in 2019, No Illusions.Through the Looking Glass, which was nominated to be considered for a Pulitzer Prize by the publisher and editor of InnerChild Press, ltd.

http://www.innerchildpress.com/jackie-davis-allen.php
jackiedavisallen.com

## Abiy Ahmed Ali

In 1976 a child was born in Beshasha, Ethiopia.
Given the name of Abiy Ahmed Ali,
He was his father's 13th child.
His mother's 6th. Her youngest.

The child grew up; longed for peace.
Resisted, militantly, against
Mengistu's communist regime.
Later, he joined the Ethiopian military.

A devout Protestant,
Abiy Ahmed's parents are deceased.
His father was a Muslim. His mother,
His father's 4th wife, was Christian Oromo.

At the age of 41, in 2017, from
Addis Ababa University, Abiy Ahmed
He completed his Ph.D; a doctorate
In peace and conflict research.

In April 2018, Abiy Ahmed
Became the fourth Prime Minister of Ethiopia.
Peace and reconciliation, always the focus.
Guided by a strong belief and faith in God.

Just one year later,
Abiy Ahmed won the 2019 Nobel Peace Prize.
How proud his wife, daughters and
Adopted son must be. His country, too.

# Something to Consider

When darkness finds light like a lost toy
And when, with its joy, a man rises
To unveil the smile of hope,
He is favored, blessed.

Mistakes invoke pain,
Yet hope sustains
If we but let love guide life into action

When man discovers friendship as a lost toy
With investment some of darkness fades.
Old mistakes rekindle pain.
Yet hope sustains.

Prayers guide fear into remission,
If we but let love's truth
Guide life into mission.

Friendship. Ah, it spreads love's light!
Its ensuing joy paints the canvas
With love, despite mistakes' shame.
Even still, hope sustains.

Effort guides man through
Various and sundry stages,
If we but allow forgiveness to guide
Love into life's mission.

# Waiting for Winter

It is cool and bright in the blue mountains.
The deep chill of night has moved, settled down
Into the valley.
> The morning sun spreads her arms
> Over and around,. Breath expressed
> With autumn's colors, it is a gift.

Still, quiet, peaceful like, I walk
Around leaves: yellow, red, rust, and brown.
Many have fallen to welcoming ground,
> Protection's blanket for nature's seedlings.
> 'Tis season's own version of a healthy need
> To relax, contemplate, to hibernate.

My heart skips to the tune of earth's blessings.
My lips are singing a song, the stanzas not formed
Neither notes upon a page  or played
> By musicians, nor ever sung
> By any, except those who dare
> To leave behind the world's loud noises.

I welcome you, O, peaceful morning.
Your gift of joy is mine.  Rest, relief you bring
To my soul.  You remind me to shine down
> And all around.  You, I embrace.
> I ask God, I pray God,
> May the world be at peace.

# Tzemin
# Ition
# Tsai

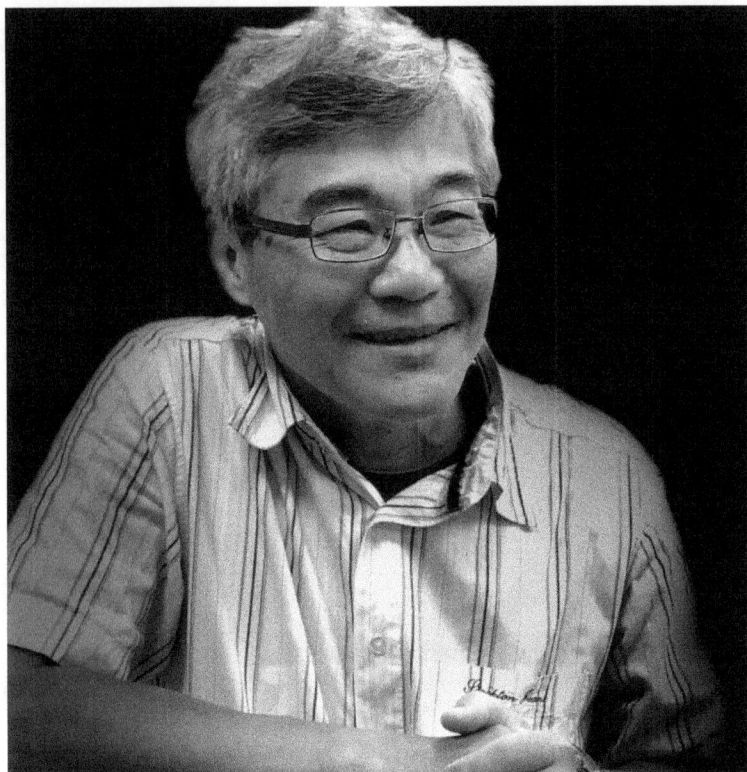

Dr. Tzemin Ition Tsai (蔡澤民博士) was born in Republic of China, in 1957. He holds a Ph.D. in Chemical Engineering and two Masters of Science in Applied Mathematics and Chemical Engineering. He is a professor at Asia University (Taiwan), editor of "Reading, Writing and Teaching" academic text. He also writes the long-term columns for Chinese Language Monthly in Taiwan.

He is a scholar with a wide range of expertise, while maintaining a common and positive interest in science, engineering and literature member. He is also an editor of "Reading, Writing and Teaching" academic text and a columnist for *'Chinese Language Monthly'* in Taiwan

He has won many national literary awards. His literary works have been anthologized and published in books, journals, and newspapers in more than 40 countries and have been translated into more than a dozen languages.

# The Danger Of Ethnic Slur

Abiyot, in the name of his childhood
That gilded and elegant handwriting asked
What should be the role of Social Capital
In Traditional Conflict Resolution?
"Doing God's work", Isn't this an answer from the heart
In the social tension caused by the conflict
A dawn of calm and peace

To allow political progress and to win people for
democracy
Response people
The asking for a different rhetoric
With an open and respectful discussion
Instead of pushing them
This seems to be an expectation that cannot be let down

Joint declaration of peace and friendship
The intoxicating and obscure light of the Nobel Peace Prize
Is it necessary or illusory?
Is it inevitable or repeated?
Increasing ethnic unrest
Barricading roads, forcibly stopping traffic to looting
Tens of thousands have been displaced from their homes
Due to ethnic based violence

Biased and vindictive
conducting ethnic profiling in the name of fighting
corruption
Daytime hyenas can't get rid of the shame of being
demarcated
Fiddled on a democratizing platform
By an opportunistic populist jockeying for power
Can even say it lightly
Occasionally can be read as euphemistic and conspiracy-
minded

# The Drunk Fisherman Who Blames The Fishing Rod Is Too Light

The waves are merciless
The canoe with short sails was attacked
The rain has no intention to
Forgave the light sails to hide from the sun was all wet
Looked at it from a distance
The poor old fisherman hiding under the canopy
With hair as pale as snow
Did he know what the boat was carrying?
Threw the bait into the depths of emerald wave with
equanimity
Let the hat on head be unfastened
The boat under feet was not anchored
Let it drift
Let it follow the waves
Asked others
What does the fisherman have?
A jug of wine
A pole of breeze
Long companioned with the sunset and reflection on a
sunny day
Long companioned with the sand gull flying

# So To Here This Dancing-Crane Town

Willow winds blow across the bank
Pairs of flying swallow's words just warmed and back to
cold again
The little flowers along the coast helped whom
To conceal the oar of the boat
Cannot bear to lose you
The stars in the sky are passing so fast
Overlooking down
The grass is green as ever between heaven and earth
Along the creek
Children crowded on the road
The chasing giggles constantly overshadowed the sound of
water
From now on
Follow the instructions of the mountains and rivers
Where can I hide without wearing noble brocade?
Look back
The deep courtyard of the Red Cloud Emperor's Palace is
located
Those past years used to shake the jade pendants
After a few simple feelings
The heart of the zither before the flowers composed the
green field into music
In exchange for a smile in the mountain where immortals
live
Like a dancing crane looking up at the sky

Shareef
Abdur
Rasheed

Shareef Abdur-Rasheed, AKA Zakir Flo was born and raised in Brooklyn, New York. His education includes Brooklyn College, Suffolk County Community College and Makkah, Saudi Arabia. He is a Veteran of the Viet Nam era, where in 1969 he reverted to his now reverently embraced Islamic Faith. He is very active in the Islamic community and beyond with his teachings, activism and his humanity.

Shareef's spiritual expression comes through the persona of "Zakir Flo" . Zakir is Arabic for "To remind". Never silent, Shareef Abdur-Rasheed is always dropping science, love, consciousness and signs of the time in rhyme.

Shareef is the Patriarch of the Abdur-Rasheed Family with 9 Children (6 Sons and 3 Daughters) and 41 Grandchildren (24 Boys and 17 Girls).

For more information about Shareef, visit his personal FaceBook Page at :

https://www.facebook.com/shareef.abdurrasheed1
https://zakirflo.wordpress.com

# Abiy

------

Ahmed you're a mover,
shaker go getter
for Ethiopian homeland
and African continent
life of service
many capacities
military, parliament,
party leader, Prime minister
reformer, serious change
government rearranges
economic reform
from state run to privatization
including major state run
essential institutions
opening up relations with
adversaries
consummate negotiator
between religious factions
Muslim/Christian conflict
facilitate resolution
in Rwanda with UN peace
force
Djibotji port agreements
bringing peace in Sudan
between north and south
especially Eritrea
stop bloody conflict
ceasefire, resolution
received 2019 Nobel
peace prize
Ethiopia, ancient Abyssinaa,

Habasha to now a land
still in tribal, factional bloody
conflict need more than ever
skillful peacemakers like
Abiy Ahmed Alii


food4thought = education

## defective
-----------
souls, hearts
of those who doubt
dem go without belief
salvation dem seek
by way of rejection
don't engage in reflection
relation of themselves
all creation
instead they're fed and
feed
anything but the truth
to convolute, deceive
even when shown
solid proof
dem deny, refute
try to explain away
why they and all
created things don't exist
in a vacuum by way
of accident

if they opened their
narrow minds they will
understand perfection
of creation
even themselves and all
things in the heavens and
earth is orchestrated
perfection should not
encounter rejection
especially when that fact
alone is manifestation

of the miracle of creation
evidence of the supreme
controlling everything
heavens, earth, birth, death
fish that swim in the sea
birds that fly in the sky
overwhelming proof
in the pudding

if only they were willing
to submit to truth
open up spiritual eyes
have souls washed
open minds
clean hearts
falsehood squashed
that can only be done
by (1) one
who made them,
everything, everyone
from where all
things come from
surely to return back again
that's a fact my friend

food4thought = education

# in the midst..,

*for the children of war*

-----------------

of carnage, destruction, genocide
but it's not you or yours going
through it
so, it's not on your mind
real life, death issues
ain't enough tissues to absorb the
tears
flowing over lands that stopped growing
in an environment of fear,
next minute might not even be there
can you be aware?
babies are aware
in reality living, thinking well beyond
their years
buried family over there
including mommy dear
dealing with horrific conditions
babies often smitten
by war
children hungry but foods no more
lost the family they adored
with memories vivid of days before
they became slaves of rage
now just a morsel of food they
crave
like the thought of reliving the days
before their family were sent to their
grave
can't help but want to bring back
those days
but can't no matter what you say

peace if there ever was, was shattered
don't try to gloss over the matter
out of sight out of mind is the matter
of course
until the horror spills on you and all
of a sudden transformed you by force
interwoven the plight of orphans
with you
because you see you in them
and sadness, concern, remorse set in
lifted you to take some action
the things you coveted no longer hold
attraction
you took them from your life via
subtraction
dealing with life and death makes one
or brakes one
like the babies who want a life but can't
get one
life's values shift under the gun
take a good hard look at yours while you
still got one
maybe you'll stop placing value on things
that have none


food4thought = education

# Kimberly Burnham

# Kimberly Burnham

A brain health expert with a PhD in Integrative Medicine, Kimberly Burnham has lived in tropical Colombia; in Belgium during the Vietnam War; in Japan teaching businessmen English; in diverse international Toronto, Canada; and several places in the US. Now, she's in Spokane, WA with her wife, Elizabeth, two sets of twins (age 11 & 14) and three dogs. Her recent book, *Awakenings: Peace Dictionary, Language and the Mind, a Daily Brain Health Program* includes the word for peace in hundreds of languages. Her poetry weaves through 80+ volumes of *The Year of the Poet, Inspired by Gandhi, Women Building the World*, and *A Woman's Place in the Dictionary*. She is currently working on several ekphrastic writing projects. One is a novel, *Art Thief Cracks Healing Code for Parkinson's Disease* and the other is non-fiction, *Using Ekphrastic Fiction Writing and Poetry to Create Interest and Promote Artists, Writers, and Poets.*

http://www.NerveWhisperer.Solutions

https://healthy-brain.medium.com/bears-at-the-window-of-climate-change-d1fb403eeaf3

# Mountainous Peace on African Roof

To soon some said
when Abiy Ahmed Ali
Ethiopian Prime Minister
won the 2019 Nobel Peace Prize

Others demanded credit to Isaias Afwerki also
President of Eritrea cooperation
at the border between
a peace agreement to end
the long "no peace, no war" stalemate

Many in Minnesota's Oromo community
say much work remains
hope ignited a better life
a brighter future all
must seek reconciliation solidarity
social justice efforts
deserve recognition encouragement
a peaceful and stable Ethiopia
helps all

# Two Ethiopian Peace Saying

"The most important thing
lay the foundation of peace"
like building a home
first thing peace
then a growing family
share in abundance

"One who is transparent
has no one against him"
act in kindness unseen
inspire out in the open
share in abundance

---

## Oromo Gadaa "Nagaa" Peace

From Ethiopia and Eritrea
to a large population in Minnesota
"Nagaya" is peace in Oromo
defended for all living things

"Alaa manni, sa'aa namni,
maatiif waatiin hundi nagayaa?"
an Oromo Gadaa demand literally
peace to the home and neighbors
cows and humans,
family and calves and all

A comprehensive sense of harmony
without tranquility of mountains
rivers and forests
no serenity to humans

No one can be an exception
each devoted transforms conflict
in collective lives

# Elizabeth E. Castillo

Elizabeth Esguerra Castillo is a multi-awarded and an Internationally-Published Contemporary Author/Poet and a Professional Writer / Creative Writer / Feature Writer / Journalist / Travel Writer from the Philippines. She has 2 published books, "Seasons of Emotions" (UK) and "Inner Reflections of the Muse", (USA). Elizabeth is also a co-author to more than 60 international anthologies in the USA, Canada, UK, Romania, India. She is a Contributing Editor of Inner Child Magazine, USA and an Advisory Board Member of Reflection Magazine, an international literary magazine. She is a member of the American Authors Association (AAA) and PEN International.

## Web links:

Facebook Fan Page

https://free.facebook.com/ElizabethEsguerraCastillo

Google Plus

https://plus.google.com/u/0/+ElizabethCastillo

# A Labyrinth of Peace

The face of change in Ethiopia

Promoting peace in their horn of Africa

Ali once said peace is our path

To solve conflicts in a civilized manner.

Unwavering commitment he showed,

And just as trees need good soil to grow

Peace needs these to flow

Promising to heal a nation,

Ali ended political repression.

## The Bareness of Trees

Misty dew drops from the sky fall
Mixing with every tears I cried,
Does it hide the pain, the grief, the loss?
Somehow it masks the emptiness of the soul.
The autumn leaves left scars at dawn
When you chose to chase the light
The bareness of trees signifies your absence
When everywhere I look,
There's no trace of your shadow
And I ask myself, would I be fine?
Every piece of music we played lingers
Bringing tears to my eyes and once again
Every breath my mind drifts to thoughts of you.
Until the last leaf falls,
Revealing the nakedness of the trees
Below an overcast sky over a downpour
The bareness of trees, branches ran dry
Unlike the welling up of tears in my eyes,
An artist can paint the sorrowful aura
Where the trees have grown on a barren land
Alas, when the sun sets again over the horizon
Until the hues of the rainbow cheers me up once more
Behind the veil where angels ascend,
I await for spring to come to witness the blooms take over
the gloom.

## Aurora

Beauteous hues from heaven
Rays of mystic light
Guiding they Divine Flight
Orbs from space
Emitting Divine Grace
I'll go to the edge of the Earth
To witness thy illumination
Angels must have sprinkled
Stardust to light thy path
When saints and Holy Ones ascend above
Or when the gods need to descend
To Earth to remind Man of his faults.
No matter how far I may roam,
Seeing you would be like coming Home.
The Divine Light shining down on me
Manifesting transcendence of my soul
When spirits haunting the night
Finally breaks free from the world's bondage,
To go back to their origin
Like a phoenix rising,
Redeeming himself out of the chains.

# Joe
# Paire

# Joe Paire

Joseph L Paire' aka Joe DaVerbal Minddancer . . .
is a quiet man, born in a time where civil liberties
were a walk on thin ice. He's been a victim of his
own shyness often sidelined in his own quest for
love. He became the observer, charting life's path.
Taking note of the why, people do what they do. His
writings oft times strike a cord with the
dormant strings of the reader. His pen the rosined
bow drawn across the mind. He comes full-frontal
or in the subtlest way, always expressing in a way
that stimulate the senses.

www.facebook.com/joe.minddancer

# Abiyut "Revolution"

In less than two years as Prime Minister
Abiy Ahmed Ali received the Noble Peace Prize
Forging a durable peace in the Horn of Africa
I was thinking about our current situation

Democratization: We are coming out of semi-authorization
Same situation as our honored Brethren, Abiy Ahmed Ali
Press censorship, empowering Women
Minister of Peace, Federal Supreme Court President
Free and fair elections

"War is the epitome of hell for all involved"
Problem solved just for agreeing to a decision
We struggle with accepting ours
Who will emerge to be the next Noble Prize recipient?

We who strive for change and human rights
We who have spent the night in oppression
Only to awaken and fight again for peace.

# Stop Signs and Seatbelts

Did you stop at the octagon?
Did you have your seatbelt on?
Is your license up to date?
Do you have your registration?
Regulations are a tad bit less than incarceration
Have your civil liberties been liberated?

Did you stop at the octagon?
Was there a four-way intersection?
Did it infringe on your right to life?
Everyone doesn't have the will to live
But you handle that steering wheel to live
You have freedom of choice to veer right or left

Did you stop at the octagon, or chose to crash it?
Wearing a mask and social distancing
Is the same as resisting oncoming traffic
It's not magic, but tragic to assume you've lost some right
Do you drive with your headlights on at night?
You have a choice, right?
Tickets for doing the wrong thing right

So why is obeying traffic laws
different than wearing a mask
remember when there were no seatbelts
they had to make a law, to protect your health
no one wanted to wear them
excuses like wrinkled suits, man we can tell them.
I missed a funeral today, one for no seatbelt
The other was covid related, too beautiful to be safe.

## Scripted Medium

Shadows created just by description
Creative wordplay to draw the eye
Righteousness brought forthwith
I tend to rush these things
Pen and paper fuel a need to canvas the area
Torn sheets of ideas strewn in anger
Erasures of escaped thoughts I was in the wrong place
Dang typo's as if they are even, they, go figure

Meanwhile as you build a mosaic from broken smiles
Erasures' and smears one misplaced verb
Damaged canvasses too much lavishness'
I relish the thought of what I'm not scribing
Using every sense plus one
Manifesting every penitent behind what I see

# hülya

# n.

# yılmaz

Professor Emerita (Humanities, Penn State, USA), hülya n. yılmaz [sic] is a published tri-lingual author, literary translator, and Director of Editing Services (Inner Child Press International, USA). Her work has appeared in numerous anthologies of global endeavors and was presented at poetry events in the U.S. and abroad. In 2018, the WIN of British Colombia, Canada honored yılmaz with a literary excellence award. Her two poems remain permanently installed in *Telepoem Booth* (USA). hülya finds it vital for everyone to understand a deeper sense of self, and writes creatively to attain a comprehensive awareness for and development of our humanity.

Writing Web Site
https://hulyanyilmaz.com/

Editing Web Site
https://hulyasfreelancing.com

# At the Year's End

Off wandered Abiy Ahmed Ali
from the town of Beshasha in central Ethiopia
into an armed struggle
against the communist regime of Mengistu,
but not before becoming a learned individual first . . .
He excelled in his studies of computer science,
leadership and economics;
earning a doctorate in peace and conflict research.

Abiy Ahmed Ali gradually climbed up the political ladder,
never forgetting his dedication to peace.
While staying true to his commitment
to result-oriented activism,
he made history in the Ethiopian parliament.
A mere eight years later, he was declared
Ethiopia's prime minister.

At the young age of 43,
this 2019 Nobel Peace Prize recipient
was rewarded for his continuous efforts
toward the achievement of peace.
Not losing his focus on international cooperation,
he persistently took initiatives which befit his nation.
The success of resolving the border conflict
with his country's neighbor, Eritrea,
proudly carries his name.

As a well-known African proverb goes,
"it takes a village to raise a child."
The child, this time, was "peace".
The "village" evidently worked hand in hand
with its leader to persuasively demand
that collective peace be delivered.

## tomorrow's hope

my car's model is Utopia
the interior is made of Dreams

i am confined to a highway
frequented by aggressors

there comes the traffic jam . . .

denials
delusions
oppression
objectification
discrimination
self-projections
obstructions of justice

to no avail . . .

my car's tires were manufactured
in a factory of universal harmony

so, i swerve around
the self-destructive bottleneck with utmost ease
and drive on while i listen to my favorite tunes on peace:
truth
reality
factuality
responsibility
accountability
integrity
honesty
dignity

skills to think critically
equality for all – unconditionally

self- and collective-empowerment
color-blind inclusivity
unity within diversity
justice for all – universally, all-inclusively

what a serene scenery!

# A Renga for Abiy Ahmed Ali

*My dear poet-friends:*
*Your collaboration is needed on this one.*
*Here is my stanza . . .*


a garden of lanterns
rugs spread on the lush grass
"peace" in all CAPS

hülya n. yılmaz

# Teresa E. Gallion

Teresa E. Gallion was born in Shreveport, Louisiana and moved to Illinois at the age of 15. She completed her undergraduate training at the University of Illinois Chicago and received her master's degree in Psychology from Bowling Green State University in Ohio. She retired from New Mexico state government in 2012.

She moved to New Mexico in 1987. While writing sporadically for many years, in 1998 she started reading her work in the local Albuquerque poetry community. She has been a featured reader at local coffee houses, bookstores, art galleries, museums, libraries, Outpost Performance Space, the Route 66 Festival in 2001 and the State of Oklahoma's Poetry Festival in Cheyenne, Oklahoma in 2004. She occasionally hosts an open mic.

Teresa's work is published in numerous Journals and anthologies. She has two CDs: *On the Wings of the Wind* and *Poems from Chasing Light.* She has published three books: *Walking Sacred Ground, Contemplation in the High Desert* and *Chasing Light.*

*Chasing Light* was a finalist in the 2013 New Mexico/Arizona Book Awards.

The surreal high desert landscape and her personal spiritual journey influence the writing of this Albuquerque poet. When she is not writing, she is committed to hiking the enchanted landscapes of New Mexico. You may preview her work at

*http://bit.ly/1aIVPNq* or *http://bit.ly/13IMLGh*

## Abiy Ahmed Ali Political Activist

Abiy Ahmed Ali is an Ethiopian politician,
4th Prime Minister of the Federal Democratic
Republic of Ethiopia, a member of the Ethiopian
Parliament and a former military intelligence officer.

As prime minister Abiy initiated political
and economic reforms and worked to obtain
peace deals in Eritrea and Sudan.
Abiy received the 2019 Nobel Peace Prize
for his work in ending the 20-year post-war
territorial stalemate between Ethiopia and Eritrea.

## Come Touch Me

Kiss me.
I want to taste your love
and feel joy
above the realm of earth.

My lips are burning for you.
I run wild in the woods
hoping to crash in your arms.

You are not awakened to my love.
Your resistance bands hold you tight
and you do not move.

Your eyes expose a story
of deep sorrow that judges
anything new as dangerous.

I am working hard to soothe you
with kind words.  Hoping
to get pass your window of sorrow
and engage the beauty you shelter.

God is here to help me find a way
to touch your heart.  I know you feel us.
I hope your protective wall melts slowly
into my arms.

# Love Folds

Love folds the body
in its last sunset.
Soul gives a wink,
catches a ride on the moon.

She spreads her arms
in the wind.
The body gently
folds into the earth.

Soul smiles
at the smooth separation
with waves of gratitude
to Spirit.

All earth substance
must return to dust.
All souls must
return home to God.

# Ashok
# K.
# Bhargava

Ashok Bhargava is a poet, writer, community activist, public speaker, management consultant and a keen photographer. Based in Vancouver, he has published several collections of his poems: Riding the Tide, Mirror of Dreams, A Kernel of Truth, Skipping Stones, Half Open Door and Lost in the Morning Calm. His poetry has been published in various literary magazines and anthologies.

Ashok is a Poet Laureate and poet ambassador to Japan, Korea and India. He is founder of WIN: Writers International Network Canada. Its main objective is to inspire, encourage, promote and recognize writers of diverse genres, artists and community leaders. He has received many accolades including Nehru Humanitarian Award for his leadership of Writers International Network Canada, Poets without Borders Peace Award for his journeys across the globe to celebrate peace and to create alliances with poets, and Kalidasa Award for creative writings.

# Early Spring
*Dedicated to Abiy Ahmed Ali*

how to restore brotherhood
after years of hostility
between the long-time foes.

with hands in loam
lay out seeds
in curated rows.

carefully water it
as the gentle mist
blows through the fingers.

persuade the afternoon sun
to guard the freshly
imbedded seeds.

let the sprouts
grow into tender vines
flower into crop

that fills
the empty stomachs with
love, peace and dignity.

# Let it be …

They will keep pouring in like sand grains
in an hourglass and slip through the fingers.

They will blow over like dust storm
if we build walls to stop them.

Ship loads of humanity will continue to cry
out loud before every sunrise on our shores.

Even if we don't want them to show up
and where else could they go.

Stop the Latino caravans and Haitian leaky boats
from seeing the glimmer of hope.

Syria, Iraq or Afghanistan: simply burn them to ashes
in the name of light.

Just a single ray of peace is plenty to fire hope
in the dark abyss of their desperation.

We can light peace
if we really want to.

We can heal the desperate
 if we want to.

# It is … As it is

My religion is humanity.
My sacrament is my breath.

My prayer is my word.
My Temple is mother Earth.

The forests are my angels.
The rivers are my blood.

My meditation is my love.
My peace is my dove.

My wisdom is to know each other.
My universe is my brother.

Caroline
'Ceri Naz'
Nazareno
Gabis

# Carolin 'Ceri' Nazareno-Gabis

Caroline 'Ceri Naz' Nazareno-Gabis, author of Velvet Passions of Calibrated Quarks, World Poetry Canada International Director to Philippines is known as a 'poet of peace and friendship', a multi-awarded poet, editor, journalist, speaker, linguist, educator, peace and women's advocate. She believes that learning other's language and culture is a doorway to wisdom.

Among her poetic belts include PANORAMA YOUTH LITERARY AWARDS 2020, 7 th Prize Winner in the 19th, 20th and 21st Italian Award of Literary Festival; Writers International Network-Canada ''Amazing Poet 2015'', The Frang Bardhi Literary Prize 2014 (Albania), the sair-gazeteci or Poet Journalist Award 2014 (Tuzla, Istanbul, Turkey) and World Poetry Empowered Poet 2013 (Vancouver, Canada). She's a featured member of Association of Women's Rights and Development (AWID), The Poetry Posse, Galaktika Poetike, Asia Pacific Writers and Translators (APWT ), Axlepino and Anacbanua.

Her poetry and children's stories have been featured in different anthologies and magazines worldwide.

Links to her works:

panitikan.ph/2018/03/30/caroline-nazareno-gabis

apwriters.org/author/ceri_naz/

www.aveviajera.org/nacionesunidasdelasletras/id1181 .html

# Peace in the Horn of Africa

*''I believe that peace is an affair of the heart. Peace is a labor of love.''*

- ***Abiy Ahmed Ali***

aWhere peace lives?
Do you find it in the midst of scriptures?
When does peace lead?
Do you take them to your heart?
What peace gives?
Does it make you whole
As brotherhood and humanity?
Why peace called peace?
Does it fill the gaps
From the wars, hatred and killings?
Is it peace, that lies between financial securities?
Is it peace that makes a family reunited?
Does peace win or lose?
When sleep find the eternal call
From the depth of understanding
And forgiving heart?

## Shamata
(revised version)

i can hear you,
from the celestial sphere of souls,
the mantra of humanity;
so i listen to my body, my mind and my heart,
drowning in placid horizons,
i can see you,
from the light particles,
spectrum and radiance
of neutron stars,
connecting all the sacred spaces,
there is clarity and balance
connecting to myself
between our destiny;
i become the sound
in the echoing, unheard lullabies,
i become the silence
from the soothing miracles
of the unruffled time.

# in between

your eyes are lights
thy lips unsealed
while kissing the sparks
of serenity
in the eve
and predawn
of your own

until everything
solely connects
deep down
yourself
within.

# Swapna
# Behera

Swapna Behera is a bilingual contemporary poet, author, translator and editor from Odisha, India. She was a teacher from 1984 to 2015. Her stories, poems and articles are widely published in National and International journals, and ezines, and are translated into different national and International languages. She has penned six books. She is the recipient of the Prestigious International Mother Language UGADI AWARD WINNER 2019. She was conferred upon the Prestigious International Poesis Award of Honor at the 2nd Bharat Award for Literature as Jury in 2015, The Enchanting Muse Award in India World Poetree Festival 2017, World Icon of Peace Award in 2017, and the Pentasi B World Fellow Poet in 2017. She is the recipient of the Prolific Poetess Award ,The Life time Achievement Award ,The Best Planner Award ,The Sahitya Shiromani Award, ATAL BIHARI BAJPAYEE Award, ATAL Award 2018 ,Global Literature Guardian Award ,International Life Time Achievement Award and the Master of Creative Impulse Award .She has received the Honoured Poet of India from the Seychelles Government accredited Literary Society Lasher one poem A NIGHT IN THE REFUGEE CAMP is translated into 60 languages .She is the Ambassador of Humanity by Hafrikan Prince Art World Africa 2018 and an official member of World Nation's Writers Union ,Kazakhstan2018. Italy, the National President for India by Hispanomundial Union of Writers (UHE), Peru, the administrator of several poetic groups, and the Cultural Ambassador for India and South Asia of Inner Child Press African is the life member of Odisha Environmental Society.

swapna.behera@gmail.com

# a word can kill; a word can heal

the Ethiopian Prime minister
the youngest influential leader in Africa
who is slow yet fast?
"democracy is unthinkable without freedom
for peace; the foundation is justice
peace is our path"

a country is the blood stream of the heart
you may be sacked from your country
but certainly, none can snatch the country from your heart
love is the need of the hour
none is perfect under the sky
if you avoid people for their mistakes
 you will be alone in the world
 known for his charisma
the young reformer served as a UN Peacekeeper in Rwanda
in the middle of the worst political and social crisis
 Kal Yigedlal, Kal yadinal
a word can kill, a word can heal
 for he unified Ethiopia and
diaspora community
a military veteran he is
for love, peace and unity
fostered internal stability,
social cohesion
his Medemer concept is addition
and coming together
 destroying hate wall
he is the noble peace laureate
Dr Abiy Ahmed Ali......

## my digital footsteps

I sing, dance and fight with my inner self
I compose, I delete
 my own protocol
the fanning breeze,
 the lotus in the pond
the cries of the starving
the helpless ones those who need me
I never see or listen
my digital footsteps trigger me to run and run the race

looking at myself in the time zone
I feel, I am the only single bird
in the horizon
stooping up and down
carrying turbid years on my wings
in due course of time become
a digital trash; so difficult to clean
I pray for a metamorphosis
instead of robotics
let me listen to the tears
 let me be an idiosyncratic composer .....

# how long ......

how long the girl beyond the hamlet will wait for a school?
how long the impotent spring will wait to celebrate?
how long shall I have to wait for a cosmic conversation?
how long shall I wait to frame love's anthem?
how long the dreams will wait to germinate?
how long someone will fight against the abuses?
how long the colours will fix the political agendas!
how long the rare and extinguished species will cry to survive?
how long the civilisation will take to stop war and terrorism?
how long the child will wait to get a park?
how long mothers will wait to feel assured for their daughters?
how long innocent smiles will be missing?
how long ......
I really mean it ......

# Albert
# 'Infinite'
# Carrasco

Albert "Infinite The Poet" Carrasco is an urban poet, mentor and public speaker.

Albert believes his experience of growing up in poverty, dealing with drugs and witnessing murder over and over were lessons learnt, in order to gain knowledge to teach. Albert's harsh reality and honesty is a powerfully packed punch delivered through rhyme. Infinite grew up in the east part of the Bronx and still resides there, so he knows many young men will follow the same dark path he followed looking for change. The life of crime should never be an option to being poor but it is, very often.

Infinite poetry @lulu.com

Alcarrasco2 on YouTube

Infinite the poet on reverbnation

# Infinite Poetry

http://www.lulu.com/us/en/shop/al-infinite-carrasco/infinite-poetry/paperback/product-21040240.html

# Abiy Ahmed Ali

Abiy Ahmed Ali was born on August 15 1976 in Beshasha
Ethiopia,
located next to Agaro, Ormia.
His father was Muslim and his mother was into
Christianity,
his entire family was religious and frequent mosque or
church attendees.
Abiy was protestant, a family of religious plurality.
Abiy Ahmed Ali is a very intellectual man,
He has a PH.D. and holds a Master of Business
Administration.
His intelligence led him to become Ethiopia's prime
Minister.
In 2019 Abiy Ahmed Ali won the Nobel Peace Prize.
His motivation was peace and international cooperation.
He as the leader in the initiative to resolve the border
conflict with Eritrea.

# Relapse

I know there's many that prayed for my downfall, I keep lettn them down. When I was hustln they wanted me to bid forever or die, now as an author they want me to get writers block and for my pen to infinitely run dry. I'll take that hate, it fuels my fire, all that does is make me set the bar higher, experience makes my bars tyta. Inf is from the birth circa, i was a hard Caine toddler, walked the walk lived the life, now I'm the game and this urban genres Godfather.

Pyrex, Gemstar and arm & hammer should sponsor my poetry because they made big money off of the team alone as we tried to mend then reinforce a broken home. Ran the streets with many men, the run was intense, the flow was immense, When I speak of most of those men, it's in past tense, I go in depth on drugs money, jail and death, if you don't know me, but hear me before reading my bio, it'll all make sense.

I'm a product of the streets and hard times, had a head start in hard knocks, as a minor my major was white crime, earned a PHD, the Power to Hear the Dead, I converse with my homies that flatlined tryna get ahead. They gave me guidance in the life of knife and slug violence, the fat lady sung death but I was tone deaf, all I heard was silence.

# Reborn

I was born in the 70's, in the 80's I was considered a crack baby, in the 2g's it was the rebirth of slick, i reinvented myself to try to save my surviving clique. A big part of my reincarnation was to save the new generation of urban sons , I use words to simulate death for those that have questions, for those thinking about hustling, read my writes of armageddon, heed my messages my bredrens, I was a bread winner like an Italian, lived the life of la costra nostra with Spanish and black brothers. a minority mafia family monopolizing with powdery ghetto commodities became a crime syndicate, plots were intricate, plans were sophisticated, movements were precisely calculated and orchestrated regardless when acted out someone became belated, we still made it. Do y'all recall want to sacrifice your man like a sacrificial lamb? Schemes were carried on even after dudes moved on, to the hungry all that meant is theres one less dude to split currency, we all knew that, we chatted bout that, gave dap saying were good money just in case that day somebody didn't come back. We were trap hustlers trap lovers, a bunch of trapped brothers relieving monetary grief from our mothers momentarily, that means until death or locked up for an eternity. I got lucky to live so I could talk about how the luck ran out for most of the kids from where I lived, to the kids from where I lived, and to all kids that live like I lived. I could educate drug counselors future drug connoisseurs and the ones who pass the LSAT to practice the 220 law. just call me a school of hard knocks professor, I'm trying to have the youth reach for excelsior instead of going to a cemetery for a move on ceremony when they pass away and yell out summa cum laude.

# Eliza Segiet

Eliza Segiet: Master's Degree in Philosophy, completed postgraduate studies in Cultural Knowledge, Philosophy, Arts and Literature at Jagiellonian University. She is a member of The Association of Polish Writers and The NWNU - Union of Writers of the World.

Her poems *Questions* and *Sea of Mists* won the title of the International Publication of the Year 2017 and 2018 in Spillwords Press.

For her volume of *Magnetic People* she won a literary award of a *Golden Rose* named after Jaroslaw Zielinski (Poland 2019 r.). Her poem The *Sea of Mists* was chosen as one of the best one hundred poems of 2018 by International Poetry Press Publication Canada.

In Poet's Yearbook, as the author of *Sea of Mists*, she was awarded with the prestigious Elite Writer's Status Award as one of the best poets of 2019 (July 2019).

She was awarded *World Poetic Star Award* by World Nations Writers Union – the world's largest Writers' Union from Kazakhstan (August 2019).

In September 2019 she was 1st Place Laureate (Foreign Poetry category) – in Contest *Quando È la Vita ad Invitare* for poem *Be Yourself* (Italy).

Her poem *Order* from volume *Unpaired* was selected as one of the 100 best poems of 2019 in International Poetry Press Publications (Canada).

Nominated for the Pushcart Prize 2019.

Nominated for the iWoman Global Awards (2019).

Laureate Naji Naaman Literary Prize 2020.

Laureate International Award PARAGON OF HOPE (Canada, 2020).

Obtained certificate of appreciation from *Gujarat Sahitya Academy* and *Motivational Strips* for literary excellence par with global standards (2020).

Ambassador of Literature granted by *Motivational Strips*.

Author's works can be found in anthologies, separate books and literary magazines worldwide.

## Spite

*To Abiy Ahmed Ali, -*
*Laureate of Nobel Peace Prize in 2019*

Not the one that was read
but the one that was lived,
the war drama
showed him, what is hell on
earth.
He was there.
Got to know bitterness of time,
of a brother killing a brother.

Luck, maybe destiny
let him live through
and create a better tomorrow.

He knew that the imaginary wall
between two countries
must be replaced by the *bridge*
*of friendship.*

Peace exists
when there is justice.
To spite hatred and discord -
—love, reconciliation, forgiveness
build harmony.


*Translated Ula de B*

# Ashes

Is this really happening?
What if
I only have such sinful dreams?

People kill animals to live,
others to…

Exactly!
Why?

I know,
they carry out orders,
breaking the laws of nature.

Nipped, I feel I am not dreaming.

There are ashes around.
An effect always has a cause.
I see the first,
I will not understand the other.


*Translated by Artur Komoter*

# Clay

We should strive to create.

Single,
strung on a thread beads
can be a decoration.
In clay
one can find an apparent life
– the shape of a formed human.

Now
we live in an upturned reality.
Some, instead of creating
– destroy,
instead of protecting
– they kill.


*Translated by Artur Komoter*

# William
# S.
# Peters Sr.

Bill's writing career spans a period of over 50 years. Being first Published in 1972, Bill has since went on to Author in excess of 50 additional Volumes of Poetry, Short Stories, etc., expressing his thoughts on matters of the Heart, Spirit, Consciousness and Humanity. His primary focus is that of Love, Peace and Understanding!

Bill says . . .

I have always likened Life to that of a Garden. So, for me, Life is simply about the Seeds we Sow and Nourish. All things we "Think and Do", will "Be" Cause and eventually manifest itself to being an "Effect" within our own personal "Existences" and "Experiences" . . . whether it be Fruit, Flowers, Weeds or Barren Landscapes! Bill highly regards the Fruits of his Labor and wishes that everyone would thus go on to plant "Lovely" Seeds on "Good Ground" in their own Gardens of Life!

to connect with Bill, he is all things Inner Child

www.iaminnerchild.com

Personal Web Site

www.iamjustbill.com

## Abiy Ahmed Ali

From the Land of Menelik and Selassie,
A land known by its Queens,
Sheba
Candace,
Amanishaketo,
Amanitore,
Shanakdakhete,
And many, many more.

……

A land
Where the scorching sands
Try the souls
Of men and women,
A land where children play games
In the realms of ideas

…….

A land of a variant and rich
Diversity of expression,
Hues and cues,
History,
Culture,
And so much more . . .

…..

There came a voice,
Filled with a wealth of insight,
Compassion,
Love,
That which only can be borne
Of the 'Mother Land' . . .
For Mother means Peace

…..

A man

Prime in stature
Who administered
Through his ministering
To the people
…..
But it was no secret,
For they, the world
Came to know him,
His spirit,
His soul,
His heart's intent,
His words
His efforts
as
Abiy Ahmed Ali

## To laugh again

It has been some time
Since I have laughed
With the abandon
I now embrace

The lunacy of the times
The absence of human rhymes
The lemons with the limes
Have given rise
As I surmise
All the things
We now say,
Conceive,
And believe

My laughter is the sugar
That makes all the nonsense
And the absence of sense
Palatable,
Yet never digestible

Isn't it all just one pisser?

I remember as a kid
When my Father tickled me
Incessantly
Because it brought us both
A certain joy,
Much like how I am tickled now
By the things
That come from the mouth
Of babes of consciousness
And fools

The word tools they employ
To divide us from our joy
Is no coy coincidence
As fences are erected
At the borders
Of our reason

The diseased season
Is upon us,
Where trust
Is a questionable paradigm
Much like those raw limes
I mentioned earlier

So, I laugh
That I may not be consumed
By the rhetoric
And misdirection,
The inflection
The selections
That beg for correction
Of the narratives

That is OK for some,
The ignorant and the plain dumb
But my friend,
We must,
Learn to laugh
And alter the collective sum
With a light of insight
That is your own,
Seek out what is known
Not the poisonous seeds
That are sown
Seek !!!! . . . .
And LEARN
To laugh again

## we are One

i removed my shoes
at the threshold
as i prepared to enter
the inner sanctum

i open that hallowed door,
i enter the House of my beloved
and i begin to de-cloak my self
of all that the world
has given me

i have cast my unified mask
of self and deceit
in the waste place
and my face is now bared

i enter the great room
where the cleansing waters run
and i begin to wash away
the accumulated soils
that reside upon the 7 skins
of my body
collected,
accumulated
from all the days
i have ever lived . . . the many life times

being pleased with my efforts
my Soul calls to me
to come to the reckoning
and i am reverent
for i have been blessed
to be able to hear

such a sweet melodious calling
and my heart begins to dance . . .
a dance i thought i had forgotten

my feet lead me down a path
adorned with the scents of becoming
and i am orgasmic with anticipation
of what is to come about

the door that is of light
the gateway that shines,
and speaks words
and incantations
of holiness and praise
opens,
and i walk in
with my head bowed
and my eyes averted
from the awe whose presence
has come for me

i am about to completely
lose my self
i am being absorbed
absolution shadows the way

there is a sense of abandon
coupled with a wanton-ness
i have never felt before,
ever
and my awareness is heightened
and overtaking
the brim
of my small cup
of self

i am ecstatic
for the air is filled
with climactic promise

i ease across the great room
to the Down tufted bed
where lovers conjugate
and i offer my self
into its soft willing embrace

i lay my self,
my weariness
my head
upon the solitary pillow
in the chamber of my betrothed

i open my self
with desire
with need
for what all Souls vie for
that i may receive the blessings
of thy seed
my sacredness calls out

the spirit of my Lover comes upon me
and captures all of my thoughts
my presence
my essence

i submit
with no recourse
for i no longer have wishes
of mine own

my vulnerabilities
are bleeding it's restraints
upon the unspoiled sheets

there is a One-ness
that comes
and consumes me
deeply
completely
and i now see clearly
through that glass
that once separated
Self from Reality
when i was but a foolish Child

i have arrived here
that i may learn to Dream
and be actualized
in all my thoughts

i will no longer speak
Dead Words,
nay . . .
i shall speak in color
with tones of a sovereignty
where chaos is enslaved to "be-ing"

this day is my day
and it is eternal

my Beloved comes to me
bathed in a robed light
that moves my perceptions
to a place
i have never been

my Lorde unveils
and stands before me
Regal
with a nakedness of wonder
that overcomes
all definitions

what do i know
for i am not thinking,
just feeling
and bathing in the flow
of the experience
which is like a gentile raging River
that can not be assuaged

i know
the Ocean of existence
is my destiny

i am ready

my consciousness is penetrated
and i am seeded with song
like that of Solomon
who too knew
of such things

my entirety begins
to quake, to quiver
and i shiver with a fulfilled knowing
that the sowing of this seed within me
shall yield a fruit
no man has ever tasted
. . . i am wasted
yet chaste

my old self
he who i once believed i knew
has dissipated
into the ether

my eyes are now closed
and my singular "I" is open
wide
and i see only 'Purpose'
and we begin to speak
of what is to come

a smile creases my face
my all-ness
filled with bliss
and the heavens open unto me
and the Angels kiss me
and all is bright
within me
and without

i fall upon my knees
offering my feeble obeisance
but there is a hand that lifts me
to my feet
and a voice commands me
and speaks unto me
to look
upon the face of thy God
there is no fear
to be found
this is Holy ground

i peer as directed
and there is a looking glass
and i see

that My God,
my Lorde
looks . . .
just like me

there is a faint whisper
a unified voice
that resonates but truth
that says to me . . .

"did you not believe
that you were made in My image ?"

"You are endowed with all that 'I AM',
and the seeds that thou have sown this day
were that of Thine own,
so be it known
that We are One."

# December 2020

## Featured Poets

~ * ~

Ratan Ghosh

Ibtisam Ibrahim al-asady

Brindha Vinodh

Selma Kopic

i Fly

because ... said the Dreamer to the world. I Can

# Ratan
# Ghosh

Ratan Ghosh (India), MPhil, PhD, an Editor, a free lance writer, a poet, a Short story writer, has experience of more than 15 years of teaching and research. He has published a number of research articles in peer review and UGC approved journal and presented seminar papers in National and International seminars in different universities of India. His poems have been featured in many international E-journals, Journals and paper back anthologies across the globe. He has edited and co-authored two international anthologies named-SUNUP and CASCADE. Recently he is editing and compiling another anthology of poems on "Gender Inequality". His poetry books like LONELY SKELETON VOL-1 and 2 and My Love: A Soul are coming soon in paperback with ISBN. His short story book "The Talisman and Other Tales" is also going to be launched in paperback.  He has received many prestigious awards for writing poetry from India and abroad. He has been awarded WORLD YOUTH ICON OF LITERATURE from NAAC, Mexico and MEWADEV LAUREL AWARD from U.P, India.

# Who can forget

Who can forget the streets?
Stained by the blood of innocent leaves
Who can forget the buds...?
Stained with the undesired clods
Who can forget the flowers?
Whose petals got withered in front of some lunatic
    powers?
Who can forget the flames of fire?
How that engulfed all the humane layers
Who can forget the shinning swords?
That beheaded the helpless veiled heads
Who can forget the long lost treasures?
Those were seized beyond measures
Who can forget the violated mothers and daughters?
Who were seized and killed without any fetters
Who can forget the long lost lands?
That had reared us without being dry and dead sands
Who can forget the borderless borders?
That had displaced and banished all from our land of
    mother
Who can forget the pains of being alien refugees?
Who had nothing but the empty sky and tears only the basic
    properties
None can forget....
Perhaps none.....
None but those who had been mysterious destitute fun
In the unknown tales of destiny...
Where the untold history sings...
The songs of mystery...
Only the songs of mystery......
Engraved for many decades in the blood stained history

# Who Shouted?

Who shouted when I was raped in front of my husband and
   sons on the way?
Who shouted when I was pierced with claws on the way?
Who shouted when my daughters were abducted on the
   way?
Who shouted when my breasts were chopped off on the
   way?
Who shouted when I was raped, gang raped and beheaded
   on the way?
Who responded when my daughters cried and called for
   help on the way?
Who shouted when our houses were looted and burnt
   without reasons?
Who shouted when our lands were forcefully seized after
   treason?
Who shouted when we had moved being unfortunate
   refugees?
Who shouted when we lost all plants and trees?
Who shouted when all men had to stand on the streets?
Who shouted when all fathers, uncles and sons had to show
   their penis?
Who shouted when they were butchered for the veiled
   penis?
Who shouted when the raped widows had to sleep with
   tears in remorse losing mental peace?
Who shouted when many winters kissed the naked, lean
   and helpless skeletons?
Who shouted when thousands killed in the Great Calcutta
   Streets?
Who shouted when mothers, daughters and sister had been
   leased?

Who shouted when many had been the burdened refugees?
Who shouted when all were banished losing voices and
    peace?
Who shouted when the country was religiously seized?
The eyes of the Eastern Beasts. . .
Only the eyes of the Eastern Beasts
But!
We were penniless . . .
We are penniless. . .
Who shout when the untold tales
Fractured, mutilated, suppressed and jailed?
Who shout when all the tales weeping for being sailed
Probably none . . .
Vote bank, healthy bank accounts and awards only
    shouting now in high pitch…
We have been the unfortunate breasts . . .
We have been the unfortunate breasts . . .
Mutilated in the untold old pages. . .
Mutilated in the untold lost pages . . .

# My Love; A Soul

Not being a fancied form…
Standing in front of thee like a violent storm
Eying, eying and eying at your downy sweet eyes
I have lost for that moment all the earthly ties
Walking through your unuttered voices I had a magical
    feel
Deep love and sincere hearts always have heavenly zeal
Unuttered uttered voices overshadow both the minds
Audibly inaudible voices never seem to know any other
    kind
I only feel your presence in my thirsty longing soul
Nothing can drift me from my desired goal
Whether you are leased or seized never do I think
Only I know how to love and how to only sink
Let us meet and sink in the vast abandoned sea
Where none but you and I will love forever in glee

Ratan Ghosh

# Ibtisam Ibrahim Al-Asady

# Ibtisam Ibrahim Al-Asady

124

Ibtisam Ibrahim al-asady
Born in Iraq Baghdad in 1980
Poet, writer and translator
Achievement:
 Bachelor of Education English Language University of
Baghdad
worked as news editor in newspapers and news websites
Trainer of English and conversation at the British Institute
of Cambridge –Al  Mansur Branch with interchange &
speak now curriculum
Trainer of English and conversation at the  institute
Academy Iraq
Member of the Association of Iraqi Translators – Baghdad
Member of the Iraqi  writers union
abtissam@ymail.com
Issues to :
 *some of my pulse 2010
*chandelier shelvings 2013
*unread messages 2014
Rapids 2017

# He was not a man

He was not a man

The one who fell from my eyes

He was not  a man

He was a saint and stripped !

# I named you Cain

The sky for your eyes...is smiling
And the birds are just for you.. singing
While me
I have grieve and silence
And the waiting for the rain
\*\*\*
Your songs flow in my heart
And on the memory's platform... fires
break out in my head
I named you Cain
Then left Abel homeless
On the door of my misery
\*\*\*
I think you mess with my thoughts
Your pigmental hand by my pains
chased my smoky thread
and on the Map of my dreams…you smile?
I named you Cain
Then my pure was assassinated
And a pride boasted on my face
then it shattered
tut for a memory.. does not contain except your name
it stops, , If I passed her
I named you Cain,
then the storm's pace has slowed
My features which I have lost in you
I still remember some of them
I still remember my face reflected..
on all the mirrors
I still remember my eyelids
At any disabled corner are hiding!

At any disabled corner are hiding!
I named you Cain.. then Abel died in my language
And my self is being Bereavement
***
I addicted your face.. Your perfume
Lovers of longing in
Addicted sky which to your eyes smiling
I addicted a chess patch in my anger
But I forgot my face reflected in all the mirrors
I named you Cain until...
the killing doesn't die into me
So the killing doesn't die into me

# I've just known ...

If the sun goes down in my lips
A thousand wishes fade away
And to attend yesterday in my language
Million letters die
And The ceiling in my isolation
Is like Sona's terrain *
I'vejust known
The God is more compassionate
When I cry
When I gloom
And The child awakes in my tears
I'vejust known...
Death does not be an autumn
Across the spectrum of challenge
I will write...
By wretched tear
all the truths
Every longing fill me out
Every flood of my glory
Every sadness smile
Appears in my entity
I will write
God has affairs do not seen
I just realized them
When I fall asleep...
when I wake up
When I gesture my fan
In the face of the hangman!


* Sona: A prison in Panama for the perpetrators
of the most heinous crimes

Ibtisam Ibrahim Al-Asady

# Brindha
# Vinodh

I hold a masters in Econometrics but I am a writer by heart. My poems and short stories have regularly appeared in magazines and ezines and newspapers.

My earliest poem was published during my school days for a magazine supporting the disabled.

My poems in an international journal and two international anthologies are due shortly.

I reside currently with my family in the United States of America.

# Misunderstanding Rendezvous with God

My eyes were caught between the edges of being asleep
and awake
like a mermaid of halves
when the cream of my dream unfurled doors of candor
to reflect upon the splendors of divine wonder.

In my rendezvous with God,
I questioned the creator about the inequalities on earth,
early deaths
and the end of the world,
the answers wrenched me...startled me to ponder.

Isn't it true that the Creator created only men and women,
aren't prejudices man-made?
Death beyond destiny the connivance of vengeance and
instinctive anxieties of revenge?
Isn't the end of the world a contemplation of contemporary
genocides?
Humans killing humans leading to a vacant land of graves?

As my eyes opened slowly to this world of uncanny
realities...
realizations aroused me from the sleep of a lost era,
a rendezvous of dream that stimulated
a dawn of diffusions scrupulous and righteous.

# A mid-night awakening

The moon a complete circle of charisma caressing
tides swinging with mood swings like rhythmic dances
amidst roads receding to retract from tiring traffic
and elegant earth enveloped in the ecstasy of eerie silence
breeze beckoning a breathtaking bliss of transient serenity
stars shimmering in shines of patterned constellations
showed suddenly the road receptacle to dwellers
when comprehensions of my complacency cuddled to finite
folds.

Road---a humble home to those homeless poor
seeking shelter with sinews strong but sullen
under the silhouetted canopy of full moon glowing through
dark lives
when my awakening was truly complete
with eyes wide open like a nocturnal bird
as speechless I stood a silent spectator
with confessions of confined capacity.

# Live today

I can't behold upon my death
the garlands of your wrapped wreath,
unwrap the bundles of your ego and warmth
to adorn me with peace while I still hold my breath.

A frozen corpse cannot lend ears
to a tribute of hitherto unshed tears,
drape me in yards of joy in the life of my years
value me if you can with a heart of spirited cheers.

# Selma
# Kopic

Selma Kopić, born in 1962 in Tuzla, Bosnia and Herzegovina. Award winner for stories and poems. The most significant is the third prize "Mak Dizdar", Stolac, BiH, 2008 for the unpublished collection of poems "Puzzle". Stories and poems have entered anthologies in Bosnia and Herzegovina and around the world. The first collection of poems is in preparation. Selma Kopić is a professor of Bosnian language and literature and lives and works in Tuzla.

# I don't know you anymore

I don't know you disarmed,
like a clay pigeon exposed.
Where are the words gone?
I don't know you weak,
like a little boy scared.
Where did the smile go?
I don't know you gentle,
as bright as the sun shone on you.
Where did the love go?
I don't know you anymore.
What you don't have, I lost too.
I don't know you anymore.
What you lost, I don't have either.

# Ne znam te više

Ne znam te razoružanog,
k'o glinenog goluba izloženog.
Gdje su nestale riječi?
Ne znam te slabog,
k'o dječačića uplašenog.
Gdje je nestao osmijeh?
Ne znam te nježnog,
k'o suncem obasjanog.
Gdje je nestala ljubav?
Ne znam te više.
Ono što ti više nemaš,
i ja sam izgubila.
Ne znam te više.
Ono što si ti izgubio,
ni ja više nemam.

# How will he find me

Don't demolish old streets or houses!
Don't close cinemas and coffee shops!
Don't cut the rows of trees!
Don't change the facades!
Once he decides to come back,
how will he find me?
What will make his heart beat faster?
What will arouse his memories
at the days he spent with me?
Is there anything sacred to you?
The street by which
he followed me home,
you turned into a cemetery!
You broke the wall
where we used to kissed!
You replaced the bench
where we hollowed out our names!
We, who are lefted our youth in this town,
do we have the right to vote,
you soulless, some new,
who knows from where, the "builders"?
Nothing is the same in this city,
no street corners, no walls, no road ...
We no longer have old places!
No more the corner where he
was waiting for me.
Nothing that will awaken his memories,
nothing that will make him to think of me,
nothing that will touch his heart,
once, when decides to come back,
he will not find.

## Kako će me naći

Ne rušite stare ulice ni kuće!
Ne zatvarajte kina ni kafiće!
Ne sijecite drvorede!
Ne mijenjajte fasade!
Kad jednom odluči da se vrati,
kako će me naći?

Šta će ga u srce taći?
Šta će mu probuditi uspomene
na dane sa mnom provedene?
Je li vam išta sveto?
Ulicu kojom me pratio
u groblje ste pretvorili!
Porušili ste zid
uz koji smo se ljubili!
zamijenili klupu na kojoj smo
svoja imena izdubili...!
Mi, koji smo mladost
u ovom ostavili gradu,
imamo li pravo glasa,
vi bezdušni, neki novi,
ko zna odakle "graditelji"?
U ovom gradu ništa više nije isto
ni uglovi ulica, ni zidovi, ni cesta...
Nemamo više stara mjesta.
Nema više ugla na kojem me čekao.
Ničeg što će probuditi uspomene,
ničeg što će ga sjetiti na mene,
ništa što će ga u srce taći,
jednom,
kad odluči da se vrati,
neće naći.

# Selma Kopic

## Thoughts intoxicated by night

I'm getting up with you and
lying with you.
I'm telling you
how I spent the day.
With the sounds of music,
shared memories awaken.
Walking through the city,
by the sight of my eyes,
I draw your attention
to the old and the new.
I put my hand over your back
when you fall asleep.
I make foam coffee for you
and cinnamon flavored fruit cake.
I am silent with you,
as your fingers crowd the pebbles
on the beach,
while you nervously croak in place
looking for the key to a problem
and combining solutions.
I look at you while you're playing,
you run your fingers through the strings,
only then seemingly calm.
I look at you as you drive and,
with the gentleness or fervor
of your movements,
I'm setting your mood.
I read your feelings
looking at your hands.
I answer your curiosity
comforting that it was caused
by desire

to get to know me better.
I promise you
that I'll get rid of bad habits
to be good enough
for you.
I struggle with that,
because I love you
just the way you are.
And,
because I love the most,
doesn't that make me
good enough?
And I wonder, over and over,
why are you crouching in place,
kneading your fingers and
asking me to change.
In the late hours of the night,
the walls and I talk to you.
We understand you.
We justify you.
We cry with you.
We cry without you.
We cry for you.
And then,
the thoughts  intoxicated by night,
become verses,
they become a poem
by which I love you,
by which I gently touch you,
by which I call you,
by which I love you.

## Misli opijene noću

Ustajem s tobom i
s tobom liježem.
Pričam ti
kako sam provela dan.
Uz zvuke muzike
uspomene zajedničke niču.
Hodajući gradom,
skrećem ti pažnju na staro i novo,
pogledom.
Stavim ti ruku preko leđa
kad umoran zaspiš.
Kafu s pjenom ti pravim i
kolač voćni s okusom cimeta.
Šutim s tobom dok ti prsti
gužvaju šljunak na plaži,
dok nervozno cupkaš u mjestu
tražeći ključ nekog problema
i kombinujući rješenja.
Gledam te dok sviraš,
prebireš prstima po žicama
jedino tada naoko smiren.
Gledam te dok voziš i
blagošću ili žestinom tvojih pokreta
odmjeravam ti raspoloženje.
Čitam osjećanja tvoja
gledajući ruke tvoje.
Odgovaram na tvoju znatiželju
tješeći se da je uzrokovana željom
da me bolje upoznaš.
Obećavam ti
da ću se riješiti loših navika
da bih bila dovoljno dobra

za tebe.
Borim se s tim jer
ja tebe volim
baš takvog kakav jesi.
I
zato što volim najviše,
zar me to ne čini
dovoljno dobrom?
I pitam se, uvijek i nanovo,
zašto cupkaš, gnječiš prste i
tražiš da se mijenjam.
U sitne sate zidovi i ja
pričamo s tobom.
Razumijemo te.
Opravdavamo te.
Plačemo s tobom.
Plačemo bez tebe.
Plačemo zbog tebe.
I onda misli
opijene noću
postaju stihovi,
postaju pjesma
kojom te volim,
kojom te milujem,
kojom te zovem,
kojom te ljubim.

# Selma Kopic

# Remembering

## our fallen soldiers of verse

*Janet Perkins Caldwell*

February 14, 1959 ~ September 20, 2016

*Alan W. Jankowski*

16 March 1961 ~ 10 March 2017

*Now available*

1 April 2020

World Healing World Peace
2020

Poets for Humanity

# Inner Child Press

## News

## Poetry Posse Members

We are so excited to share and announce a few of the current books, as well as the new and upcoming books of some of our Poetry Posse authors.

On the following pages we present to you ...

Jackie Davis Allen

Gail Weston Shazor

hülya n. yılmaz

Nizar Sartawi

Faleeha Hassan

Fahredin Shehu

Caroline 'Ceri' Nazareno

Eliza Segiet

Teresa E. Gallion

William S. Peters, Sr.

*Now Available at*
www.innerchildpress.com

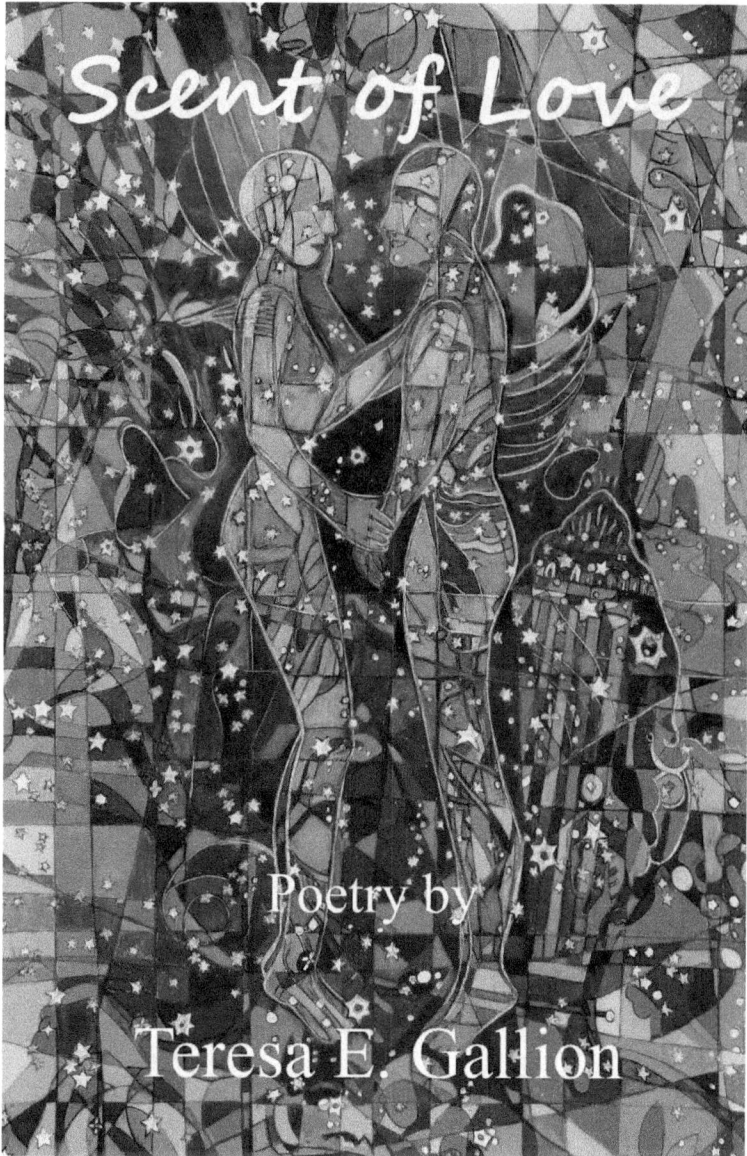

Scent of Love

Poetry by

Teresa E. Gallion

*Now Available*

www.innerchildpress.com

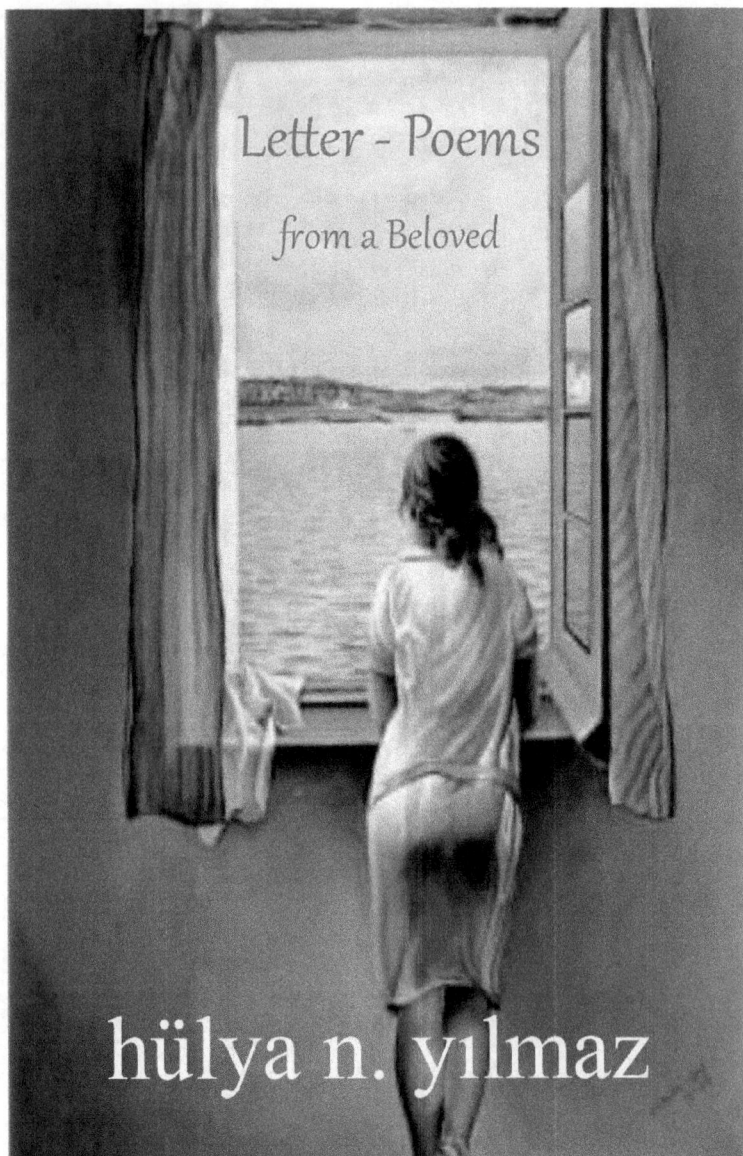

Letter - Poems

from a Beloved

hülya n. yılmaz

## Now Available
### www.innerchildpress.com

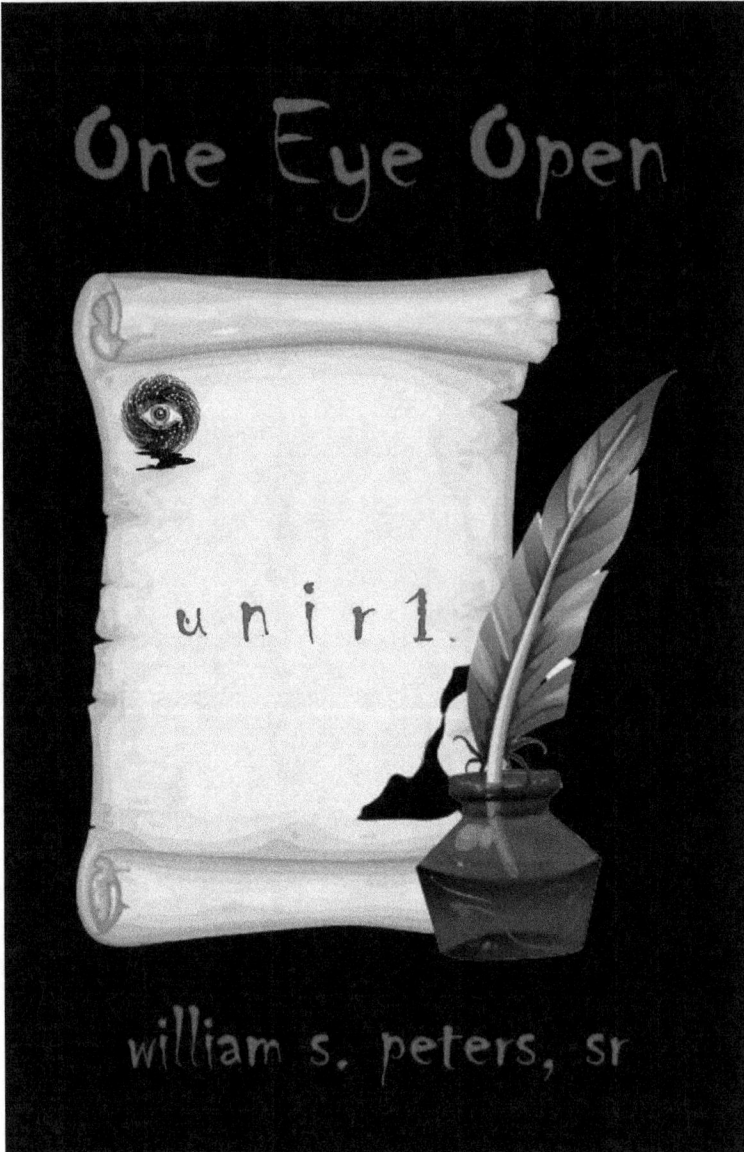

COMING SOON
www.innerchildpress.com

The Book of krisar

volume v

william s. peters, sr.

# The Book of krisar

## Volume I

william s. peters, sr.

# The Book of krisar

## Volume II

william s. peters, sr.

*Now Available*

*www.innerchildpress.com*

# The Book of krisar

Volume III

william s. peters, sr.

# The Book of krisar

Volume IV

william s. peters, sr.

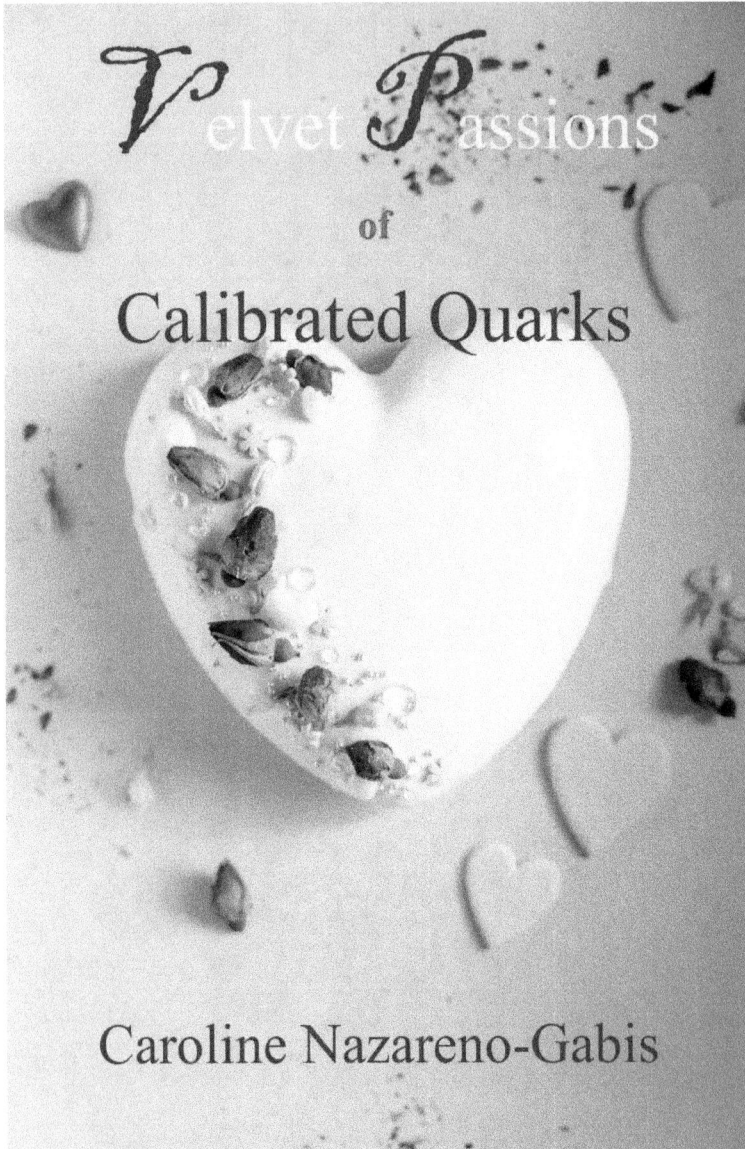

# *V*elvet *P*assions
## of
# Calibrated Quarks

## Caroline Nazareno-Gabis

Now Available

www.innerchildpress.com

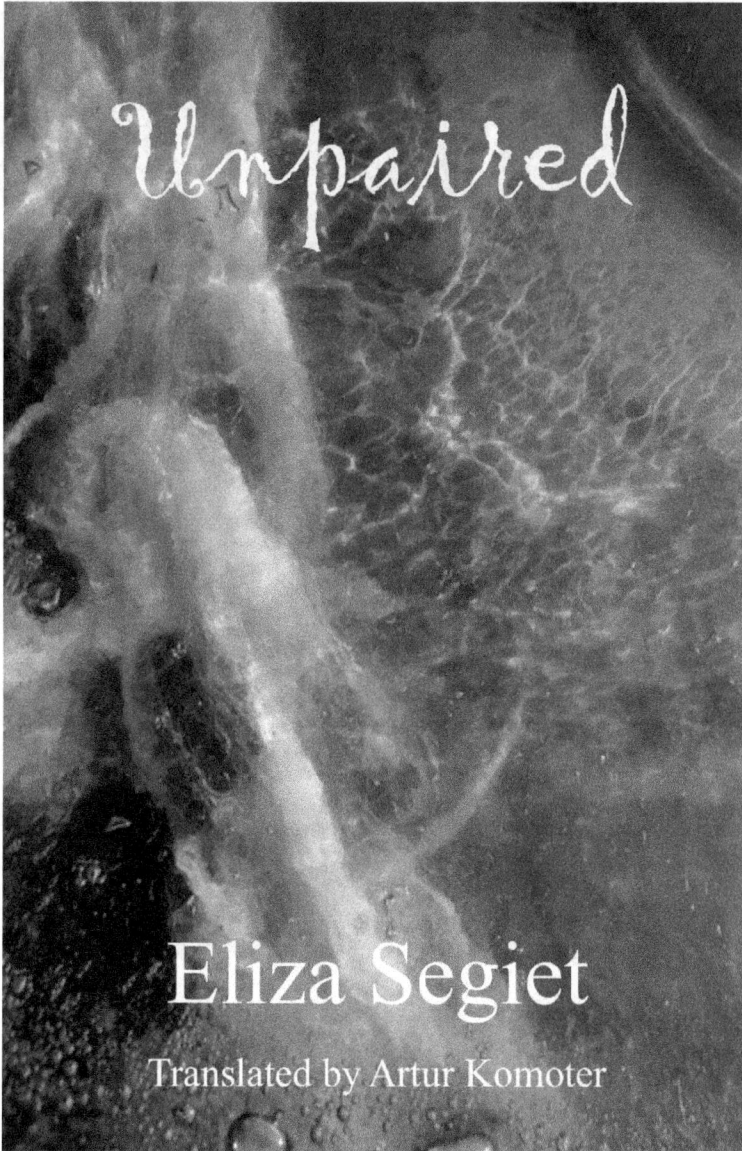

Unpaired

Eliza Segiet

Translated by Artur Komoter

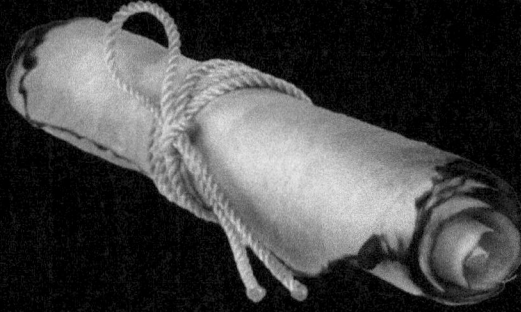

Canlarım
My Lifeblood

*poetry in Turkish and English*

hülya n. yılmaz

Now Available

www.innerchildpress.com

Butterfly's Voice

Faleeha Hassan

Translated by William M. Hutchins

*Inner Child Press News*

## Now Available at
www.innerchildpress.com

# No Illusions

*Through the Looking Glass*

Jackie Davis Allen

Now Available at
www.innerchildpress.com

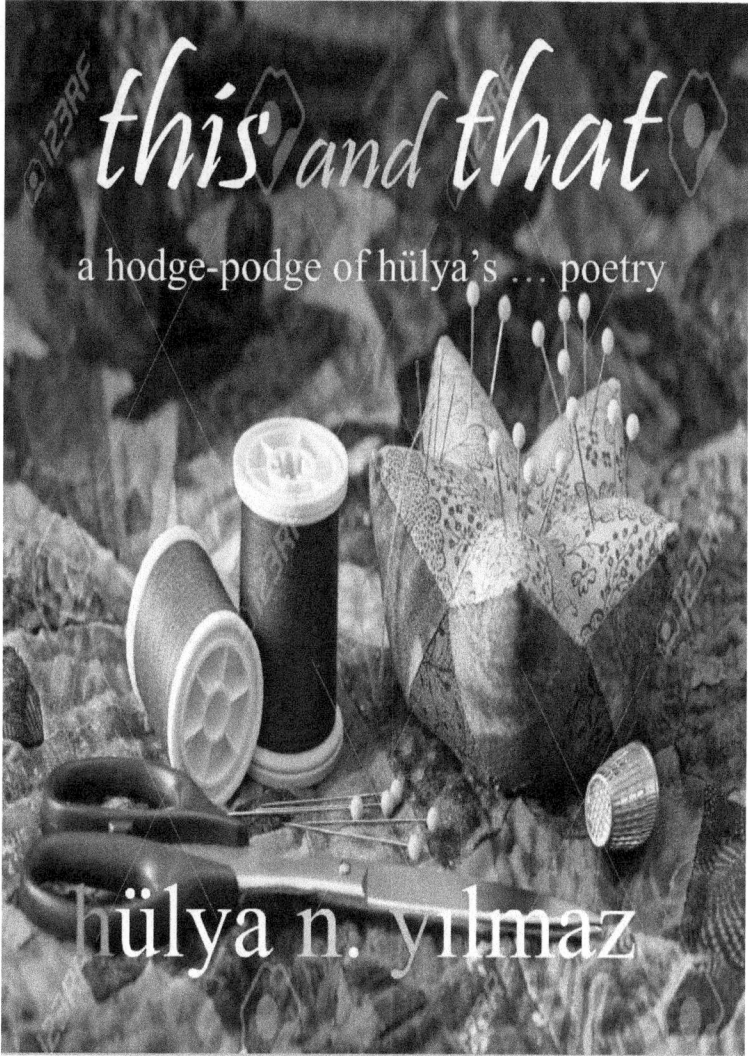

*this and that*

a hodge-podge of hülya's ... poetry

hülya n. yılmaz

**Now Available at**

*www.innerchildpress.com*

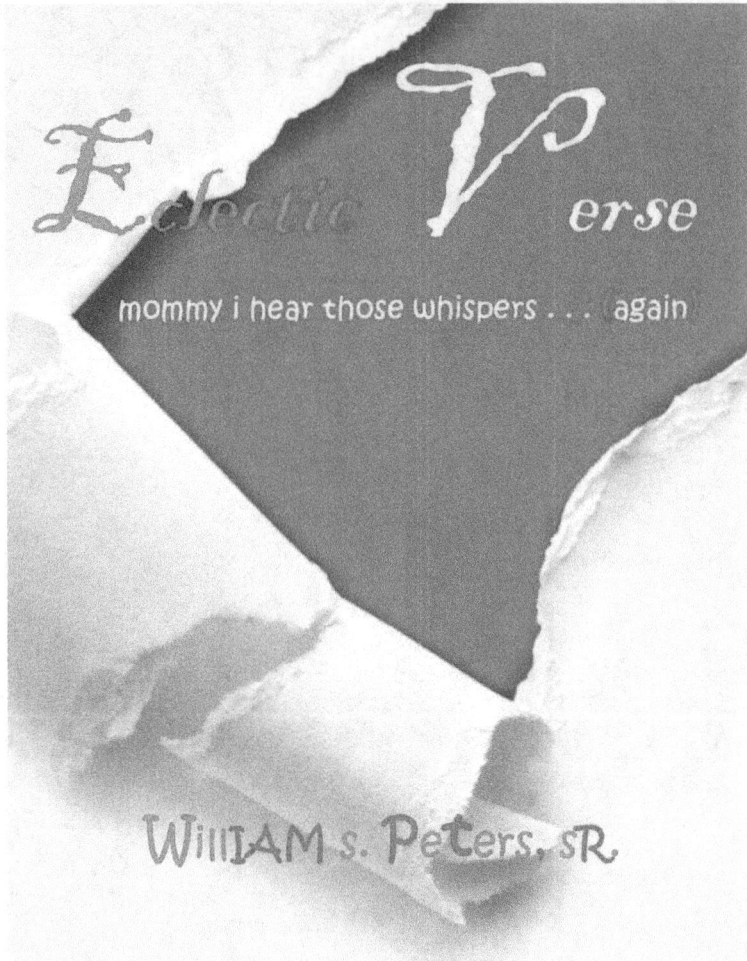

Now Available at
www.innerchildpress.com

# HERENOW

FAHREDIN SHEHU

*Inner Child Press News*

**Now Available at**
www.innerchildpress.com

Magnetic People

Eliza Segiet

Translated by Artur Komoter

Now Available at
www.innerchildpress.com

Dark Side
of the
Moon

Jackie Davis Allen

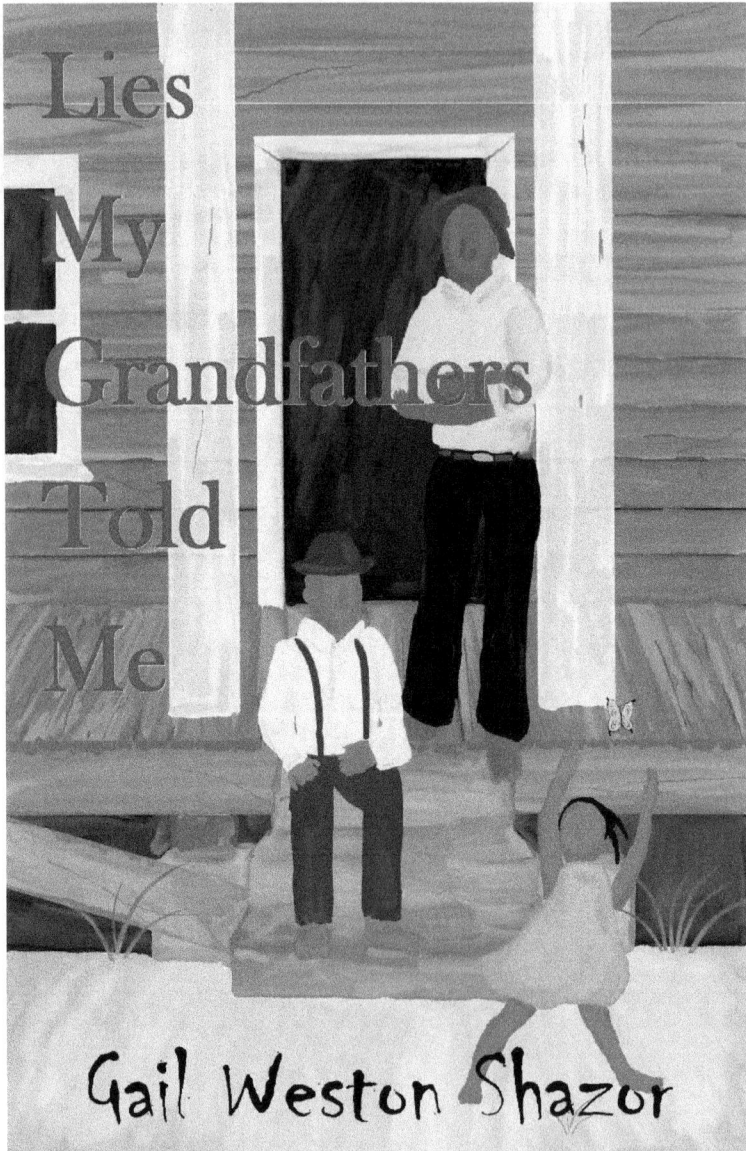

Now Available at
www.innerchildpress.com

Aflame

Memoirs in Verse

hülya n. yılmaz

My Shadow

Nizar Sartawi

Now Available at
www.innerchildpress.com

Mass Graves

Faleeha Hassan

*Inner Child Press News*

**Now Available at**
**www.innerchildpress.com**

# Breakfast

for

# Butterflies

## Faleeha Hassan

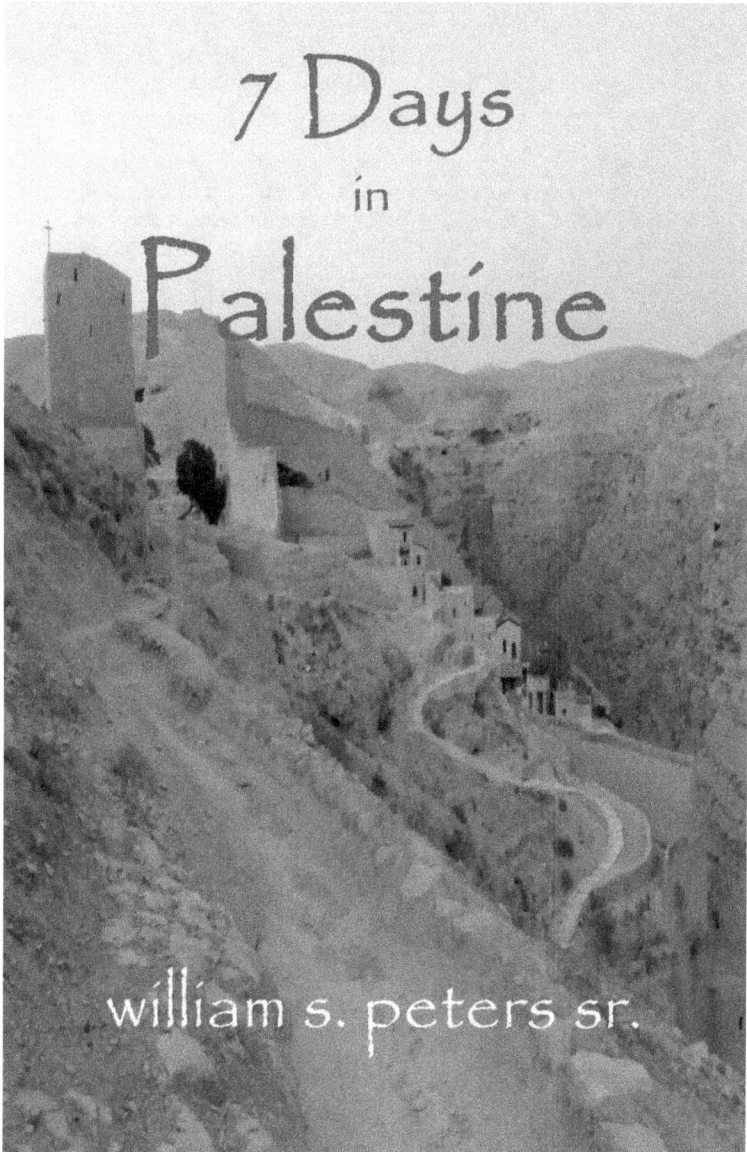

# 7 Days in Palestine

william s. peters sr.

**Now Available at**

www.innerchildpress.com

inner child press
presents

*Tunisia My Love*

william s. peters, sr.

Now Available at

www.innerchildpress.com

INNER CHILD PRESS

THIS IS WHY I
SLEEP

william s. peters sr.

Inward Reflections

This could work...

Yes...

I got it...

Ohh...

Think on These Things
*Book II*

# william s. peters, sr.

# Other

# Anthological

## works from

Inner Child Press International

www.innerchildpress.com

# World Healing World Peace
## 2020

## Poets for Humanity

*Now Available*

www.worldhealingworldpeacepoetry.com

Inner Child Press International
&
The Year of the Poet
present

# Poetry

*the best of 2020*

## Poets of the World

*Coming December 2020*
*www.innerchildpress.com*

Inner Child Press International

*presents*

# W.A.R.

*We Are Revolution*

*Poets for Humanity*

*Now Available*
www.innerchildpress.com

the **H**eart of a **P**oet

words for a better tomorrow

## The Conscious Poets

*Now Available*

*www.innerchildpress.com*

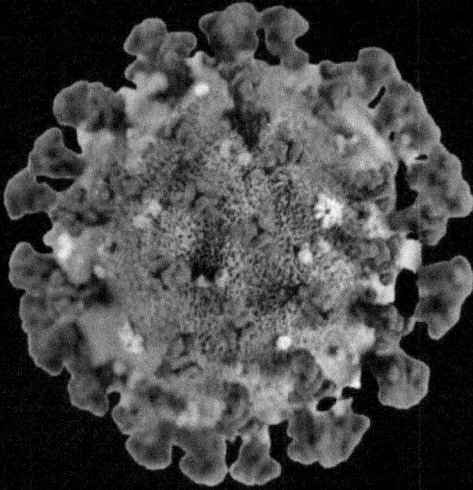

*Now Available*
*www.innerchildpress.com*

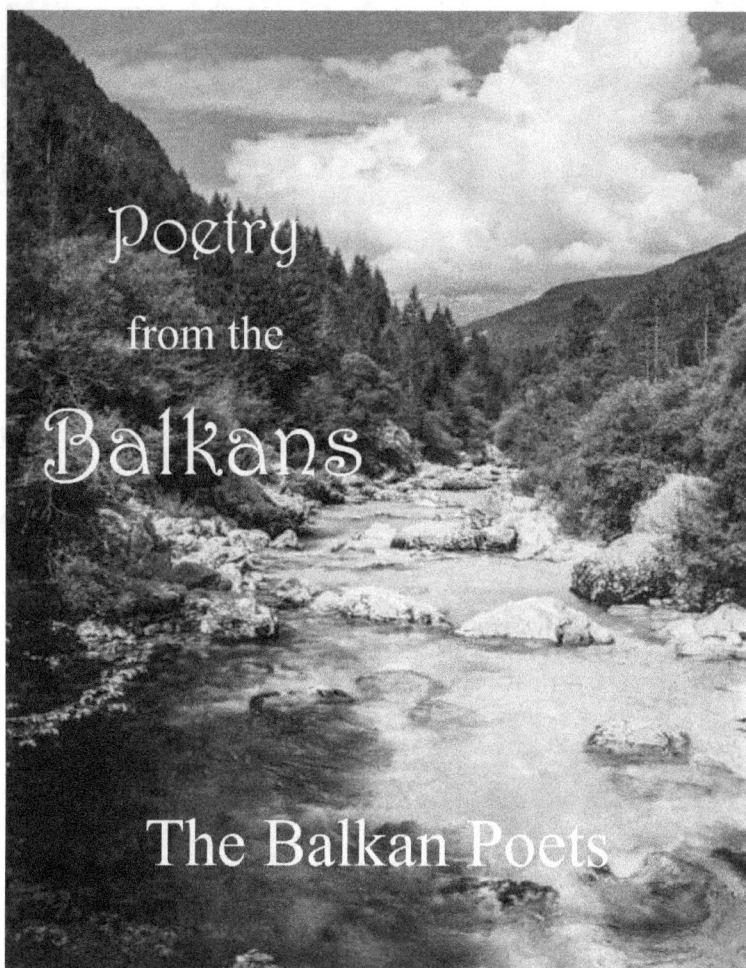

Poetry
from the
Balkans

The Balkan Poets

*Now Available at*
*www.innerchildpress.com*

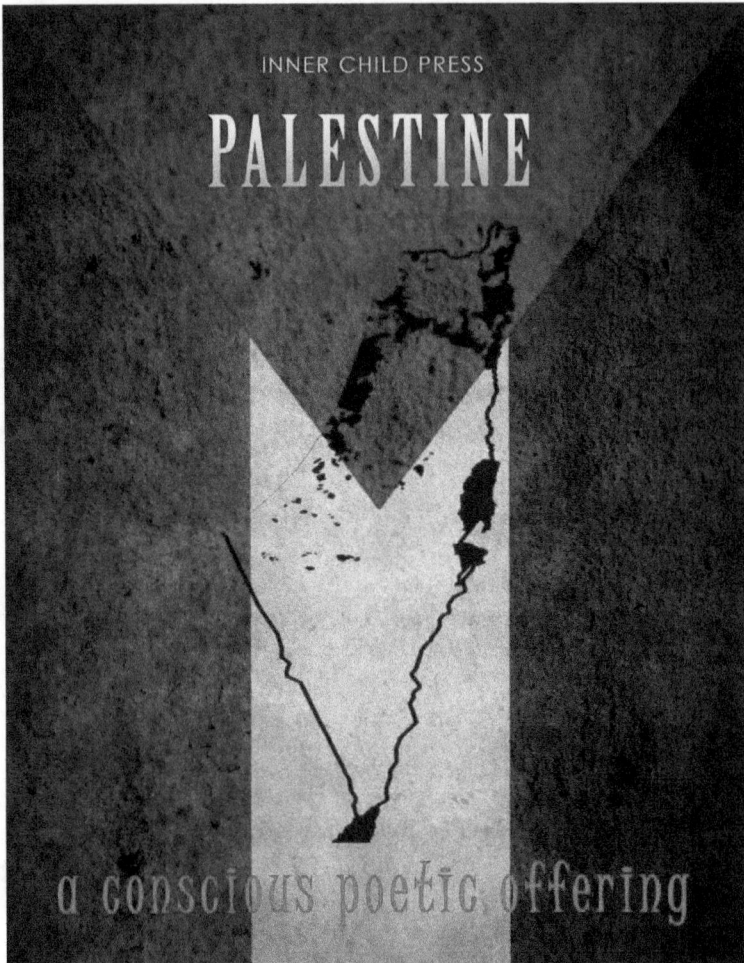

INNER CHILD PRESS

# PALESTINE

a conscious poetic offering

*Now Available at*
*www.innerchildpress.com*

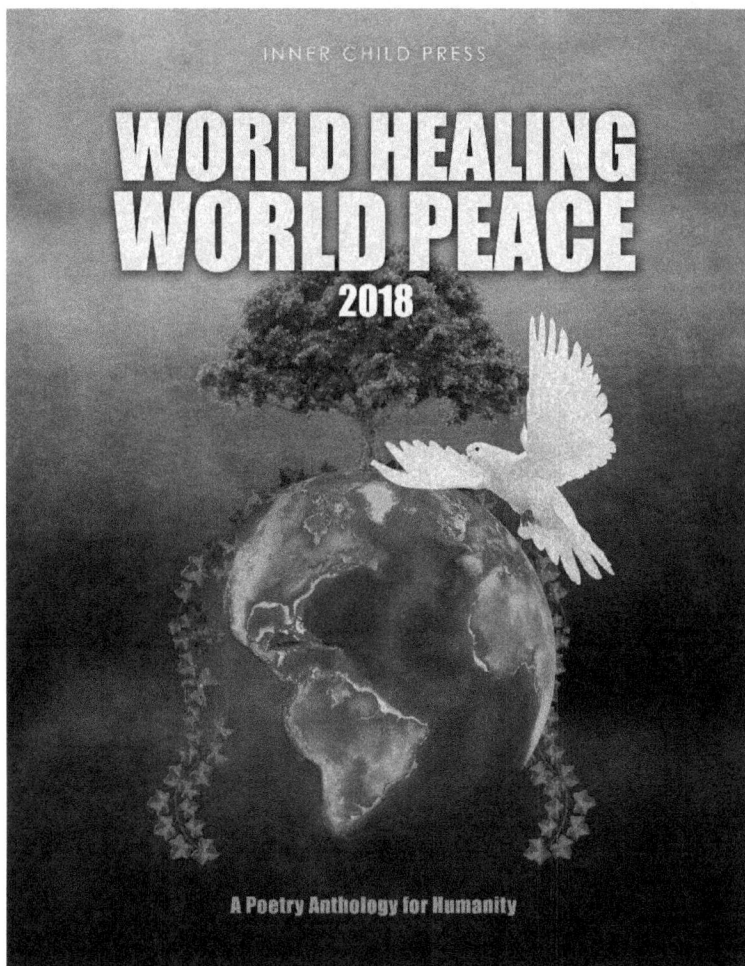

INNER CHILD PRESS

# WORLD HEALING WORLD PEACE
## 2018

A Poetry Anthology for Humanity

*Now Available at*
*www.innerchildpress.com*

Inner Child Press International
*presents*

# A Love Anthology

2019

The Love Poets

*Now Available*

www.worldhealingworldpeacepoetry.com

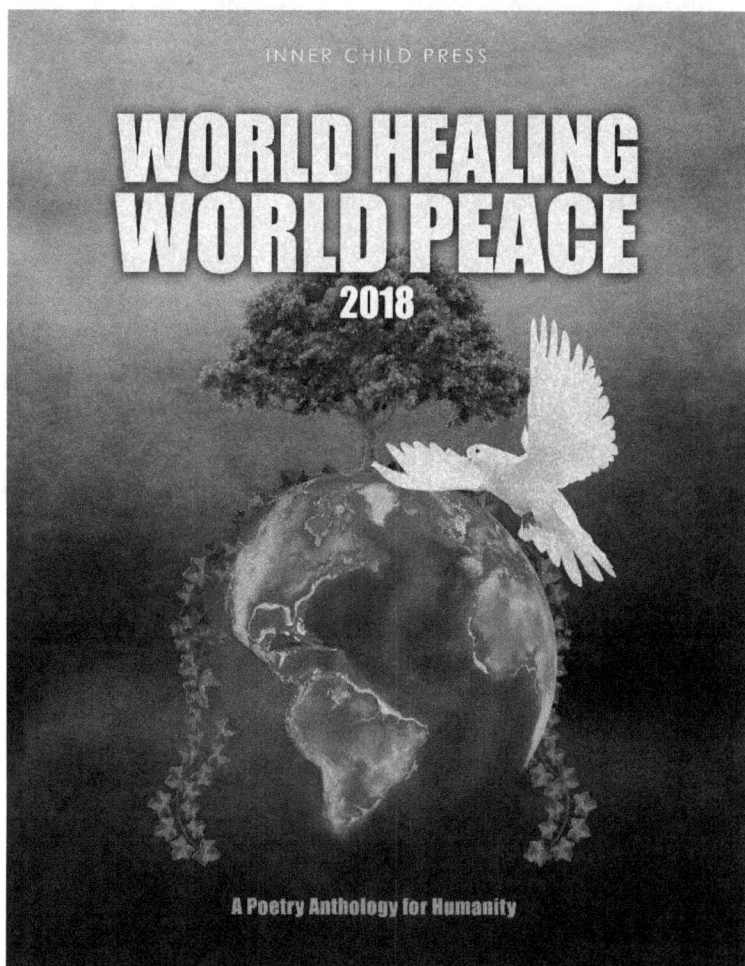

INNER CHILD PRESS

# WORLD HEALING WORLD PEACE
## 2018

A Poetry Anthology for Humanity

*Now Available*

www.worldhealingworldpeacepoetry.com

*Now Available*

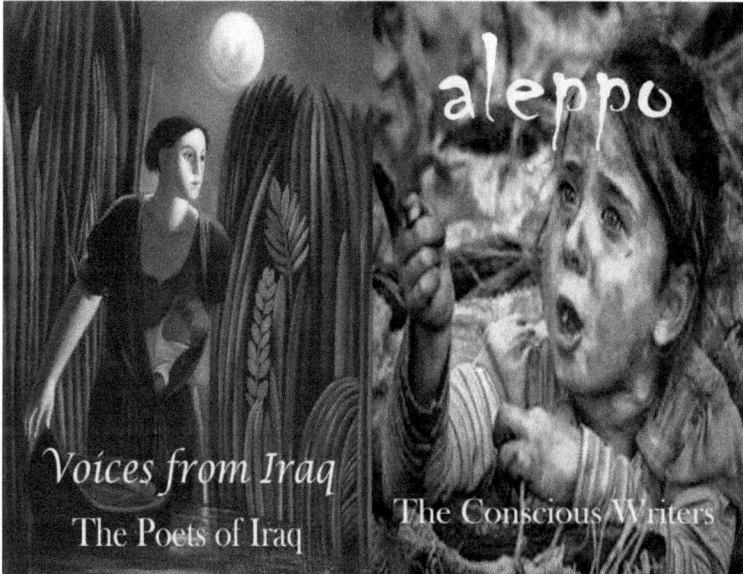

Now Available

www.innerchildpress.com/anthologies

Now Available

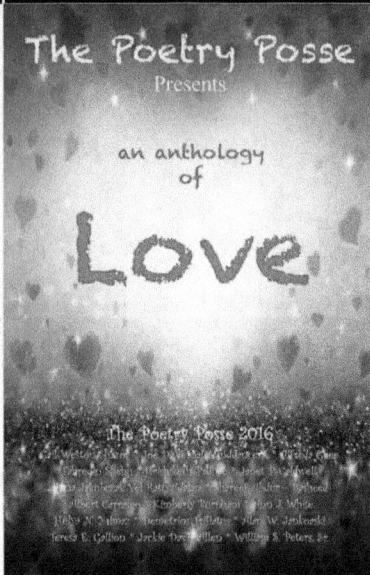

## Now Available

www.innerchildpress.com/anthologies

# Inner Child Press Anthologies

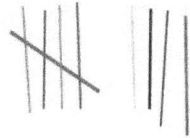

(9 lines . . .)

*for those who are challenged*

*an anthology of Poetry inspired by . . .*

Poetry Dancer

## Now Available

www.innerchildpress.com/anthologies

## The Year of the Poet
### January 2014

**The Poetry Posse**

Jamie Bond
Gail Weston Shazor
Albert 'Infinite' Carrasco
Siddartha Beth Pierce
Janet P. Caldwell
June 'Bugg' Barefield
Debbie M. Allen
Tony Henninger
Joe DaVerbal Minddancer
Robert Gibbons
Neetu Wali
Shareef Abdur-Rasheed
William S. Peters, Sr.

Carnation

*Our January Feature*
**Terri L. Johnson**

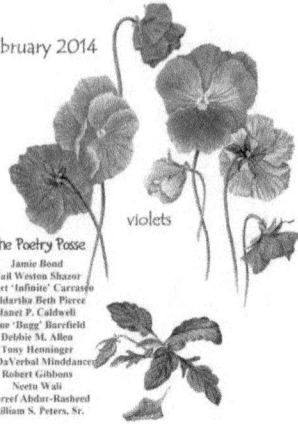

## the Year of the Poet

February 2014

violets

**The Poetry Posse**

Jamie Bond
Gail Weston Shazor
Albert 'Infinite' Carrasco
Siddartha Beth Pierce
Janet P. Caldwell
June 'Bugg' Barefield
Debbie M. Allen
Tony Henninger
Joe DaVerbal Minddancer
Robert Gibbons
Neetu Wali
Shareef Abdur-Rasheed
William S. Peters, Sr.

*Our February Features*
Teresa E. Gallion & Robert Gibson

## the Year of the Poet

March 2014

The Poetry Posse
Jamie Bond
Gail Weston Shazor
Albert 'Infinite' Carrasco
Siddartha Beth Pierce
Janet P. Caldwell
June 'Bugg' Barefield
Debbie M. Allen
Tony Henninger
Joe DaVerbal Minddancer
Robert Gibbons
Neetu Wali
Shareef Abdur-Rasheed
Kimberly Burnham
William S. Peters, Sr.

daffodil

*Our March Featured Poets*
Alicia C. Cooper & hülya yılmaz

## the Year of the Poet

April 2014

The Poetry Posse
Jamie Bond
Gail Weston Shazor
Albert 'Infinite' Carrasco
Siddartha Beth Pierce
Janet P. Caldwell
June 'Bugg' Barefield
Debbie M. Allen
Tony Henninger
Joe DaVerbal Minddancer
Robert Gibbons
Neetu Wali
Shareef Abdur-Rasheed
Kimberly Burnham
William S. Peters, Sr.

*Our April Featured Poets*
Fahredin Shehu
Martina Reisz Newberry
Justin Blackburn
Monte Smith

Sweet Pea

celebrating international poetry month

## Now Available

www.innerchildpress.com/the-year-of-the-poet

the year of the poet
May 2014

May's Featured Poets
ReeCee
Joski the Poet
Shannon Stanton

Dedicated to our Children

The Poetry Posse
Jamie Bond
Gail Weston Shazor
Albert 'Infinite' Carrasco
Siddartha Beth Pierce
Janet P. Caldwell
June 'Bugg' Barefield
Debbie M. Allen
Tony Henninger
Joe DaVerbal Minddancer
Robert Gibbons
Neetu Wali
Kareef Abdur-Rasheed
Kimberly Burnham
William S. Peters, Sr.

Lily of the Valley

the Year of the Poet
June 2014

Love & Relationship

Rose

June's Featured Poets
Shantelle McLin
Jacqueline D. E. Kennedy
Abraham N. Benjamin

The Poetry Posse
Jamie Bond
Gail Weston Shazor
Albert Infinite' Carrasco
Siddartha Beth Pierce
Janet P. Caldwell
June 'Bugg' Barefield
Debbie M. Allen
Tony Henninger
Joe DaVerbal Minddancer
Robert Gibbons
Neetu Wali
Shareef Abdur-Rasheed
Kimberly Burnham
William S. Peters, Sr.

The Year of the Poet
July 2014

July Feature Poets
Christena A. V. Williams
Dr. John R. Strum
Kolade Olanrewaju Freedom

The Poetry Posse
Jamie Bond
Gail Weston Shazor
Albert 'Infinite' Carrasco
Siddartha Beth Pierce
Janet P. Caldwell
June 'Bugg' Barefield
Debbie M. Allen
Tony Henninger
Joe DaVerbal Minddancer
Robert Gibbons
Neetu Wali
Shareef Abdur-Rasheed
Kimberly Burnham
William S. Peters, Sr.

Lotus
Asian Flower of the Month

The Year of the Poet
August 2014

Gladiolus

The Poetry Posse
Jamie Bond
Gail Weston Shazor
Albert Infinite' Carrasco
Siddartha Beth Pierce
Janet P. Caldwell
June 'Bugg' Barefield
Debbie M. Allen
Tony Henninger
Joe DaVerbal Minddancer
Robert Gibbons
Neetu Wali
Shareef Abdur-Rasheed
Kimberly Burnham
William S. Peters, Sr.

August Feature Poets
Ann White • Rosalind Cherry • Shella Jenkins

Now Available

www.innerchildpress.com/the-year-of-the-poet

197

Inner Child Press Anthologies

The Year of the Poet
September 2014

Aster          Morning-Glory

Wild Child of Silent Men Blooms Flower

September Feature Poets
Florence Malone * Keith Alan Hamilton

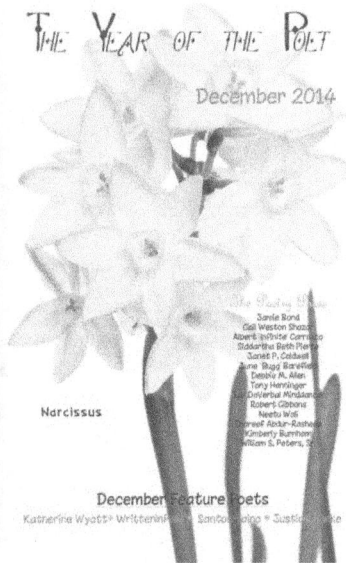

The Poetry Posse
Jamie Bond * Gail Weston Shazor * Albert 'Infinite' Carrasco * Siddartha Beth Pierce
Janet P. Caldwell * June 'Bugg' Barefield * Debbie M. Allen * Tony Henninger
Joe DaVerbal Minddancer * Robert Gibbons * Neetu Wali * Shareef Abdur-Rasheed
Kimberly Burnham * William S. Peters, Sr.

THE YEAR OF THE POET
October 2014

Red Poppy

The Poetry Posse
Jamie Bond * Gail Weston Shazor * Albert 'Infinite' Carrasco * Siddartha Beth Pierce
Janet P. Caldwell * June 'Bugg' Barefield * Debbie M. Allen * Tony Henninger
Joe DaVerbal Minddancer * Robert Gibbons * Neetu Wali * Shareef Abdur-Rasheed
Kimberly Burnham * William S. Peters, Sr.

October Feature Poets
Ceri Naz * Rajendra Padhi * Elizabeth Castillo

THE YEAR OF THE POET
November 2014

Chrysanthemum

The Poetry Posse
Jamie Bond * Gail Weston Shazor * Albert 'Infinite' Carrasco * Siddartha Beth Pierce
Janet P. Caldwell * June 'Bugg' Barefield * Debbie M. Allen * Tony Henninger
Joe DaVerbal Minddancer * Robert Gibbons * Neetu Wali * Shareef Abdur-Rasheed
Kimberly Burnham * William S. Peters, Sr.

November Feature Poets
Jocelyn Mosman * Jackie Allen * James Moore * Neville Hiatt

THE YEAR OF THE POET
December 2014

Narcissus

The Poetry Posse
Jamie Bond
Gail Weston Shazor
Albert Infinite Carrasco
Siddartha Beth Pierce
Janet P. Caldwell
June 'Bugg' Barefield
Debbie M. Allen
Tony Henninger
DaVerbal Minddancer
Robert Gibbons
Neetu Wali
Shareef Abdur-Rasheed
Kimberly Burnham
William S. Peters, Sr.

December Feature Poets
Katherina Wyatt * Writteninpink * Santorella Ringo * Justice Cole

Now Available

www.innerchildpress.com/the-year-of-the-poet

198

## THE YEAR OF THE POET II
### January 2015

Garnet

The Poetry Posse

Jamie Bond
Gail Weston Shazor
Albert 'Infinite' Carrasco
Siddartha Beth Pierce
Janet P. Caldwell
Tony Henninger
Joe DaVerbal Minddancer
Robert Gibbons
Neetu Wali
Shareef Abdur - Rasheed
Kimberly Burnham
Ann White
Keith Alan Hamilton
Katherine Wyatt
Fahredin Shehu
Hülya N. Yılmaz
Teresa E. Gallion
Jackie Allen
William S. Peters, Sr.

January Feature Poets
Bismay Mohanti * Jen Walls * Eric Judah

## THE YEAR OF THE POET II
### February 2015

Amethyst

THE POETRY POSSE

Jamie Bond
Gail Weston Shazor
Albert 'Infinite' Carrasco
Siddartha Beth Pierce
Janet P. Caldwell
Tony Henninger
Joe DaVerbal Minddancer
Robert Gibbons
Neetu Wali
Shareef Abdur - Rasheed
Kimberly Burnham
Ann White
Keith Alan Hamilton
Katherine Wyatt
Fahredin Shehu
Hülya N. Yılmaz
Teresa E. Gallion
Jackie Allen
William S. Peters, Sr.

FEBRUARY FEATURE POETS
Iram Fatima * Bob McNeil * Kerstin Centervall

## The Year of the Poet II
### March 2015

Our Featured Poets
Heung Sook * Anthony Arnold * Alicia Foland

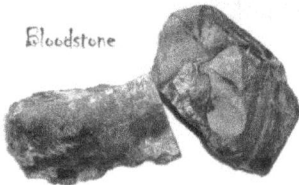

Bloodstone

The Poetry Posse 2015
Jamie Bond * Gail Weston Shazor * Albert 'Infinite' Carrasco
Siddartha Beth Pierce * Janet P. Caldwell * Tony Henninger
Joe DaVerbal Minddancer * Neetu Wali * Shareef Abdur - Rasheed
Kimberly Burnham * Ann White * Keith Alan Hamilton
Katherine Wyatt * Fahredin Shehu * Hülya N. Yılmaz
Teresa E. Gallion * Jackie Allen * William S. Peters, Sr

## The Year of the Poet II
### April 2015

Celebrating International Poetry Month

Our Featured Poets
Raja Williams * Dennis Ferado * Laure Charazac

Diamonds

The Poetry Posse 2015
Jamie Bond * Gail Weston Shazor * Albert 'Infinite' Carrasco
Siddartha Beth Pierce * Janet P. Caldwell * Tony Henninger
Joe DaVerbal Minddancer * Neetu Wali * Shareef Abdur - Rasheed
Kimberly Burnham * Ann White * Keith Alan Hamilton
Katherine Wyatt * Fahredin Shehu * Hülya N. Yılmaz
Teresa E. Gallion * Jackie Allen * William S. Peters, Sr.

## Now Available

www.innerchildpress.com/the-year-of-the-poet

## The Year of the Poet II
### May 2015

May's Featured Poets
Geri Algeri
Akin Mosi Chinnery
Anna Jakubczak

Emeralds

The Poetry Posse 2015
Jamie Bond • Gail Weston Shazor • Albert 'Infinite' Carrasco
Siddartha Beth Pierce • Janet P. Caldwell • Tony Henninger
Joe DaVerbal Minddancer • Neetu Wali • Shareef Abdur – Rasheed
Kimberly Burnham • Ann White • Keith Alan Hamilton
Katherine Wyatt • Fahredin Shehu • Hülya N. Yılmaz
Teresa E. Gallion • Jackie Allen • William S. Peters, Sr.

## The Year of the Poet II
### June 2015

June's Featured Poets
Anahit Arustamyan • Yvette D. Murrell • Regina A. Walker

Pearl

The Poetry Posse 2015
Jamie Bond • Gail Weston Shazor • Albert 'Infinite' Carrasco
Siddartha Beth Pierce • Janet P. Caldwell • Tony Henninger
Joe DaVerbal Minddancer • Neetu Wali • Shareef Abdur – Rasheed
Kimberly Burnham • Ann White • Keith Alan Hamilton
Katherine Wyatt • Fahredin Shehu • Hülya N. Yılmaz
Teresa E. Gallion • Jackie Allen • William S. Peters, Sr.

## The Year of the Poet II
### July 2015

The Featured Poets for July 2015
Abhik Shome • Christina Neal • Robert Neal

Rubies

The Poetry Posse 2015
Jamie Bond • Gail Weston Shazor • Albert 'Infinite' Carrasco
Siddartha Beth Pierce • Janet P. Caldwell • Tony Henninger
Joe DaVerbal Minddancer • Neetu Wali • Shareef Abdur – Rasheed
Kimberly Burnham • Ann White • Keith Alan Hamilton
Katherine Wyatt • Fahredin Shehu • Hülya N. Yılmaz
Teresa E. Gallion • Jackie Allen • William S. Peters, Sr.

## The Year of the Poet II
### August 2015

Peridot

Featured Poets
Gayle Howell
Ann Chalasz
Christopher Schultz

The Poetry Posse 2015
Jamie Bond • Gail Weston Shazor • Albert 'Infinite' Carrasco
Siddartha Beth Pierce • Janet P. Caldwell • Tony Henninger
Joe DaVerbal Minddancer • Neetu Wali • Shareef Abdur – Rasheed
Kimberly Burnham • Ann White • Keith Alan Hamilton
Katherine Wyatt • Fahredin Shehu • Hülya N. Yılmaz
Teresa E. Gallion • Jackie Allen • William S. Peters, Sr.

*Now Available*

www.innerchildpress.com/the-year-of-the-poet

## The Year of the Poet II

September 2015

### Featured Poets

Alfreda Ghee · Lonneice Weeks Badley · Demetrios Trifiatis

Sapphires

The Poetry Posse 2015

Jamie Bond * Gail Weston Shazor * Albert 'Infinite' Carrasco
Siddartha Beth Pierce * Janet P. Caldwell * Tony Henninger
Joe DaVerbal Minddancer * Neetu Wali * Shareef Abdur – Rasheed
Kimberly Burnham * Ann White * Keith Alan Hamilton
Katherine Wyatt * Fahredin Shehu * Hülya N. Yılmaz
Teresa E. Gallion * Jackie Allen * William S. Peters, Sr.

## The Year of the Poet II

October 2015

### Featured Poets

Monte Smith * Laura J. Wolfe * William Washington

Opal

The Poetry Posse 2015

Jamie Bond * Gail Weston Shazor * Albert 'Infinite' Carrasco
Siddartha Beth Pierce * Janet P. Caldwell * Tony Henninger
Joe DaVerbal Minddancer * Neetu Wali * Shareef Abdur – Rasheed
Kimberly Burnham * Ann White * Keith Alan Hamilton
Katherine Wyatt * Fahredin Shehu * Hülya N. Yılmaz
Teresa E. Gallion * Jackie Allen * William S. Peters, Sr.

## The Year of the Poet II

November 2015

### Featured Poets

Alan W. Jankowski
Ihisay Mohanty
James Mowe

Topaz

The Poetry Posse 2015

Jamie Bond * Gail Weston Shazor * Albert 'Infinite' Carrasco
Siddartha Beth Pierce * Janet P. Caldwell * Tony Henninger
Joe DaVerbal Minddancer * Neetu Wali * Shareef Abdur – Rasheed
Kimberly Burnham * Ann White * Keith Alan Hamilton
Katherine Wyatt * Fahredin Shehu * Hülya N. Yılmaz
Teresa E. Gallion * Jackie Allen * William S. Peters, Sr.

## The Year of the Poet II

December 2015

### Featured Poets

Kerione Bryan * Michelle Joan Barulich * Neville Hiatt

Turquoise

The Poetry Posse 2015

Jamie Bond * Gail Weston Shazor * Albert 'Infinite' Carrasco
Siddartha Beth Pierce * Janet P. Caldwell * Tony Henninger
Joe DaVerbal Minddancer * Neetu Wali * Shareef Abdur – Rasheed
Kimberly Burnham * Ann White * Keith Alan Hamilton
Katherine Wyatt * Fahredin Shehu * Hülya N. Yılmaz
Teresa E. Gallion * Jackie Allen * William S. Peters, Sr.

## Now Available

www.innerchildpress.com/the-year-of-the-poet

The Year of the Poet III
January 2016

Featured Poets
Lana Joseph * Atom Cyrus Rush * Christena Williams

Dark-eyed Junco

The Poetry Posse 2016

The Year of the Poet III
February 2016

Featured Poets
Anthony Arnold
Anna Chalasz
Andre Hawthorne

Puffin

The Poetry Posse 2016

The Year of the Poet
March 2016

Featured Poets
Jeton Kelmendi   Nizar Sartawi   Sami Muhanna

Robin

The Poetry Posse 2016

The Year of the Poet III

Featured Poets
Ali Abdolrezaei
Anna Chalasz
Agim Vinca
Ceri Naz

Black Capped Chickadee

The Poetry Posse 2016

celebrating international poetry month

# Now Available

www.innerchildpress.com/the-year-of-the-poet

The Year of the Poet
May 2016

Bob Strum
Barbara Allan
D.L. Davis

Oriole

The Year of the Poet III
June 2016

Featured Poets

Qibrije Demiri- Frangu
Naime Beqiraj
Faleeha Hassan
Bedri Zyberaj

Black Necked Stilt

The Poetry Posse 2016

Year of the Poet I
July

Iram Fatima 'Ashi
Langley Shazor
Jody Doty
Emilia I. Davis

Indigo Bunting

The Poetry Posse 2016

The Year of the Poet III
August 2016

Featured Poets

Anita Dash
Irena Jovanovic
Malgorzata Gouluda

Painted Bunting

The Poetry Posse 2016

Now Available

www.innerchildpress.com/the-year-of-the-poet

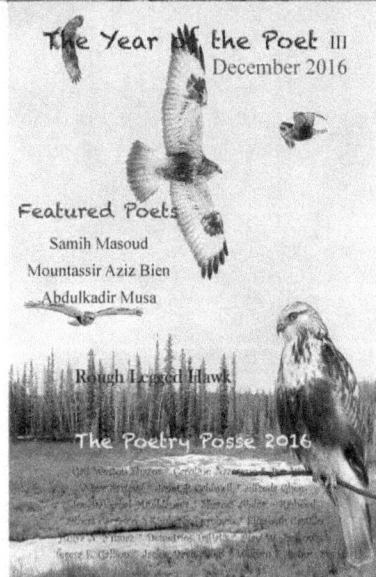

**Now Available**

www.innerchildpress.com/the-year-of-the-poet

The Year of the Poet IV
January 2017

Featured Poets
Jon Winell
Natalie Shields
Irani Fatima Aski

Quaking Aspen

The Poetry Posse 2017

Gail Weston Shazor * Caroline Nazareno * Ramey Mohanty
Nizar Sartawi * Hanz Jakobczak Vel Ratty Adalan * Jen Walls
Joe DeVerhal Middlerone * Shareef Abdur – Rasheed
Albert Carrasco * Kimberly Burnham * Elizabeth Castillo
Hülya N. Yılmaz * Falesha Hooper * Alex W. Jankowski
Teresa E. Gallion * Jackie Davis Allen * William S. Peters, Sr.

The Year of the Poet IV
February 2017

Featured Poets
Lin Ross
Soukaina Fathi
Anwer Ghani

Witch Hazel

The Poetry Posse 2017

Gail Weston Shazor * Caroline Nazareno * Ramey Mohanty
Nizar Sartawi * Hanz Jakobczak Vel Ratty Adalan * Jen Walls
Joe DeVerhal Middlerone * Shareef Abdur – Rasheed
Albert Carrasco * Kimberly Burnham * Elizabeth Castillo
Hülya N. Yılmaz * Falesha Hooper * Alex W. Jankowski
Teresa E. Gallion * Jackie Davis Allen * William S. Peters, Sr.

The Year of the Poet IV
March 2017

Featured Poets
Tremell Stevens
Francisca Ricinski
Jamit Abu Shaih

The Eastern Redbud

The Poetry Posse 2017

Gail Weston Shazor * Caroline Nazareno * Ramey Mohanty
Teresa E. Gallion * Hanz Jakobczak Vel Ratty Adalan
Joe DeVerhal Middlerone * Shareef Abdur – Rasheed
Albert Carrasco * Kimberly Burnham * Elizabeth Castillo
Hülya N. Yılmaz * Falesha Hooper * Jackie Davis Allen
Jen Walls * Nizar Sartawi * William S. Peters, Sr.

The Year of the Poet IV
April 2017

Featured Poets
Dr. Rachida Barnous
Neptune Bartram
Masood Khabi

The Blossoming Cherry

The Poetry Posse 2017

Gail Weston Shazor * Caroline Nazareno * Ramey Mohanty
Nizar Sartawi * Hanz Jakobczak Vel Ratty Adalan
Joe DeVerhal Middlerone * Shareef Abdur – Rasheed
Albert Carrasco * Kimberly Burnham * Elizabeth Castillo
Hülya N. Yılmaz * Falesha Hooper * Jackie Davis Allen
Jen Walls * Nizar Sartawi * William S. Peters, Sr.

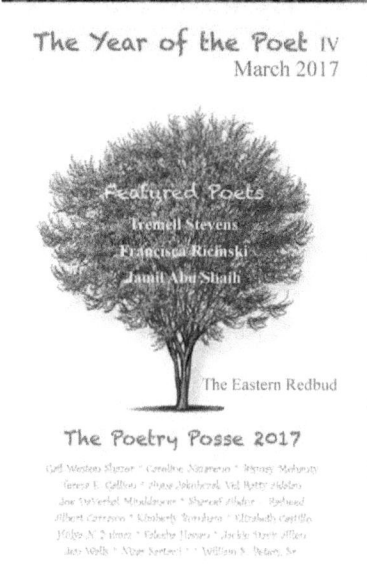

# Now Available

www.innerchildpress.com/the-year-of-the-poet

## The Year of the Poet IV
September 2017

### Featured Poets

Martina Reisz Newberry
Ameer Nassir
Christine Fulco Neal
Robert Neal

The Elm Tree

### The Poetry Posse 2017

Gail Weston Shazor * Caroline Nazareno * Bismay Mohanty
Teresa E. Gallion * Anna Jakubczak Vel Ratty Adalan
Joe DaVerbal Minddancer * Shareef Abdur – Rasheed
Albert Carrasco * Kimberly Burnham * Elizabeth Castillo
Hülya N. Yılmaz * Faleeha Hassan * Jackie Davis Allen
Jen Walls * Nizar Sartawi * * William S. Peters, Sr.

## The Year of the Poet IV
October 2017

### Featured Poets

**Ahmed Abu Saleem**
**Nedal Al-Qaeim**
**Sadeddin Shahin**

The Black Walnut Tree

### The Poetry Posse 2017

Gail Weston Shazor * Caroline Nazareno * Bismay Mohanty
Teresa E. Gallion * Anna Jakubczak Vel Ratty Adalan
Joe DaVerbal Minddancer * Shareef Abdur – Rasheed
Albert Carrasco * Kimberly Burnham * Elizabeth Castillo
Hülya N. Yılmaz * Faleeha Hassan * Jackie Davis Allen
Jen Walls * Nizar Sartawi * * William S. Peters, Sr.

## The Year of the Poet IV
November 2017

### Featured Poets

Kay Peters
Alfreda D. Ghee
Gabriella Garofalo
Rosemary Cappello

The Tree of Life

### The Poetry Posse 2017

Gail Weston Shazor * Caroline Nazareno * Bismay Mohanty
Teresa E. Gallion * Anna Jakubczak Vel Ratty Adalan
Joe DaVerbal Minddancer * Shareef Abdur – Rasheed
Albert Carrasco * Kimberly Burnham * Elizabeth Castillo
Hülya N. Yılmaz * Faleeha Hassan * Jackie Davis Allen
Jen Walls * Nizar Sartawi * William S. Peters, Sr.

## The Year of the Poet IV
December 2017

### Featured Poets

Justice Clarke
Mariel M. Pabroa
Kiley Brown

The Fig Tree

### The Poetry Posse 2017

Gail Weston Shazor * Caroline Nazareno * Bismay Mohanty
Teresa E. Gallion * Anna Jakubczak Vel Ratty Adalan
Joe DaVerbal Minddancer * Shareef Abdur – Rasheed
Albert Carrasco * Kimberly Burnham * Elizabeth Castillo
Hülya N. Yılmaz * Faleeha Hassan * Jackie Davis Allen
Jen Walls * Nizar Sartawi * William S. Peters, Sr.

## Now Available

www.innerchildpress.com/the-year-of-the-poet

The Year of the Poet V
January 2018
Featured Poets
Iyad Shamasnah
Yasmeen Hamzeh
Ali Abdolrezaei

Aksum

The Poetry Posse 2018
Gail Weston Shazor * Caroline Nazareno * Tezmin Ition Tsai
Hülya N. Yılmaz * Faleeha Hassan * Jackie Davis Allen
Teresa E. Gallion * Anna Jakubczak Vel Ratty Adalan
Alicja Maria Kuberska * Shareef Abdur – Rasheed
Kimberly Burnham * Elizabeth Castillo
Nizar Sartawi * William S. Peters, Sr.

The Year of the Poet V
February 2018

Sabean

Featured Poets
Muhammad Azram
Anna Szawracka
Abhilipsa Kuanar
Aanika Aery

The Poetry Posse 2018
Gail Weston Shazor * Caroline Nazareno * Tezmin Ition Tsai
Hülya N. Yılmaz * Faleeha Hassan * Jackie Davis Allen
Teresa E. Gallion * Anna Jakubczak Vel Ratty Adalan
Alicja Maria Kuberska * Shareef Abdur – Rasheed
Kimberly Burnham * Elizabeth Castillo
Nizar Sartawi * William S. Peters, Sr.

The Year of the Poet V
March 2018

Featured Poets
Irara Fatima "Ashi"
Cassandra Swan
Jaleel Khazaal
Shazia Zaman

Caribbean
&
Middle America

The Poetry Posse 2018
Gail Weston Shazor * Nizar Sartawi * Hülya N. Yılmaz
Jackie Davis Allen * Caroline "Ceri" Nazareno
Alicja Maria Kuberska * Teresa E. Gallion
Faleeha Hassan * Shareef Abdur – Rasheed
Kimberly Burnham * Elizabeth Castillo
Tezmin Ition Tsai * William S. Peters, Sr.

The Year of the Poet V
April 2018

Featured Poets

The Nez Perce

The Poetry Posse 2018

Now Available

www.innerchildpress.com/the-year-of-the-poet

208

The Year of the Poet V
May 2018

Featured Poets
Zaldy Carrerol de León Jr.
Sylwia K. Malinowska
Lyudila Ahmeti
Ofelia Prodan

The Sumerians

The Poetry Posse 2018

Gail Weston Shazor * Nizar Sartawi * Hülya N. Yılmaz
Jackie Davis Allen * Caroline 'Ceri' Nazareno
Alicja Maria Kubenska * Teresa E. Gallion
Kimberly Burnham * Shareef Abdur – Rasheed
Faleeha Hassan * Elizabeth Castillo * Swapna Behera
Tezmin Ition Tsai * William S. Peters, Sr.

The Year of the Poet V
June 2018

Featured Poets
Bilall Maliqi * Daim Miftari * Gojko Božović * Sofija Živković

The Paleo Indians

The Poetry Posse 2018

Gail Weston Shazor * Nizar Sartawi * Hülya N. Yılmaz
Jackie Davis Allen * Caroline 'Ceri' Nazareno
Alicja Maria Kubenska * Teresa E. Gallion
Kimberly Burnham * Shareef Abdur – Rasheed
Faleeha Hassan * Elizabeth Castillo * Swapna Behera
Tezmin Ition Tsai * William S. Peters, Sr.

The Year of the Poet V
July 2018

Featured Poets
Padmaja Iyengar-Paddy
Mohammad Bilal Hamd
Eliza Segiet
Tom Higgins

Oceania

The Poetry Posse 2018

Gail Weston Shazor * Nizar Sartawi * Hülya N. Yılmaz
Jackie Davis Allen * Caroline 'Ceri' Nazareno
Alicja Maria Kubenska * Teresa E. Gallion
Kimberly Burnham * Shareef Abdur – Rasheed
Faleeha Hassan * Elizabeth Castillo * Swapna Behera
Tezmin Ition Tsai * William S. Peters, Sr.

The Year of the Poet V
August 2018

Featured Poets
Hussein Habasch * Mircea Dan Duta * Naida Mujkić * Swagat Das

The Lapita

The Poetry Posse 2018

Gail Weston Shazor * Nizar Sartawi * Hülya N. Yılmaz
Jackie Davis Allen * Caroline 'Ceri' Nazareno
Alicja Maria Kubenska * Teresa E. Gallion
Kimberly Burnham * Shareef Abdur – Rasheed
Ashok K. Bhargava* Elizabeth Castillo * Swapna Behera
Tezmin Ition Tsai * William S. Peters, Sr.

Now Available

www.innerchildpress.com/the-year-of-the-poet

Inner Child Press Anthologies

## The Year of the Poet VI
### January 2019

Indigenous North Americans

Featured Poets

Houda Elfchtali
Anthony Briscoe
Iram Fatima 'Ashi'
Dr. K. K. Mathew

Dream Catcher

The Poetry Posse 2019

Gail Weston Shazor * Joe Paire * Hülya N. Yılmaz
Jackie Davis Allen * Caroline Cori Nazareno
Alicja Maria Kubeńska * Teresa E. Gallion
Kimberly Burnham * Shareef Abdur - Rasheed
Ashok K. Bhargava * Elizabeth Castillo * Swapna Behera
Tezmin Ituar Tsai * William S. Peters, Sr.

## The Year of the Poet VI
### February 2019

Featured Poets

Marek Łukaszewicz * Bharati Nayak
Alda G. Roque * Jean-Jacques Fournier

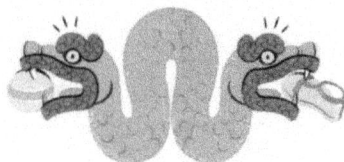

Meso-America

The Poetry Posse 2019

Gail Weston Shazor * Albert Carrasco * Hülya N. Yılmaz
Jackie Davis Allen * Caroline Nazareno * Eliza Segiet
Alicja Maria Kubeńska * Teresa E. Gallion * Joe Paire
Kimberly Burnham * Shareef Abdur – Rasheed
Ashok K. Bhargava * Elizabeth Castillo * Swapna Behera
Tezmin Ituar Tsai * William S. Peters, Sr.

## The Year of the Poet VI
### March 2019

Featured Poets

Enesa Mahmić * Sylvia K. Malinowska
Shurouk Hammoud * Anwer Ghani

The Caribbean

The Poetry Posse 2019

Gail Weston Shazor * Albert Carrasco * Hülya N. Yılmaz
Jackie Davis Allen * Caroline Nazareno * Eliza Segiet
Alicja Maria Kubeńska * Teresa E. Gallion * Joe Paire
Kimberly Burnham * Shareef Abdur – Rasheed
Ashok K. Bhargava * Elizabeth Castillo * Swapna Behera
Tezmin Ituar Tsai * William S. Peters, Sr.

## The Year of the Poet VI
### April 2019

Featured Poets

DL Davis * Michelle Joan Barulich
Lulëzim Haziri * Faleeha Hassan

Central & West Africa

The Poetry Posse 2019

Gail Weston Shazor * Albert Carrasco * Hülya N. Yılmaz
Jackie Davis Allen * Caroline Nazareno * Eliza Segiet
Alicja Maria Kubeńska * Teresa E. Gallion * Joe Paire
Kimberly Burnham * Shareef Abdur – Rasheed
Ashok K. Bhargava * Elizabeth Castillo * Swapna Behera
Tezmin Ituar Tsai * William S. Peters, Sr.

# Now Available

www.innerchildpress.com/the-year-of-the-poet

211

The Year of the Poet VI
May 2019

Featured Poets
Emad Al-Haydary * Hussein Nasser Jabr
Wahab Sheriff * Abdul Razzaq Al Ameeri

Asia Southeast Asia and Maritime Asia

The Poetry Posse 2019

Gail Weston Shazor * Albert Carrasco * Hülya N. Yılmaz
Jackie Davis Allen * Caroline Nazareno * Eliza Segiet
Alicja Maria Kuberska * Teresa E. Gallion * Joe Paire
Kimberly Burnham * Shareef Abdur – Rasheed
Ashok K. Bhargava * Elizabeth Castillo * Swapna Behera
Tezmin Ition Tsai * William S. Peters, Sr.

The Year of the Poet VI
June 2019

Featured Poets
Kate Gaudi Powiekszone * Sahaj Sabharwal
Iwu Jeff * Mohamed Abdel Aziz Shmeis

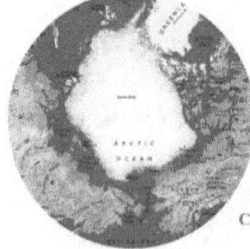

Arctic
Circumpolar

The Poetry Posse 2019

Gail Weston Shazor * Albert Carrasco * Hülya N. Yılmaz
Jackie Davis Allen * Caroline Nazareno * Eliza Segiet
Alicja Maria Kuberska * Teresa E. Gallion * Joe Paire
Kimberly Burnham * Shareef Abdur – Rasheed
Ashok K. Bhargava * Elizabeth Castillo * Swapna Behera
Tezmin Ition Tsai * William S. Peters, Sr.

The Year of the Poet VI

Featured Poets
Saudeddin Shahin   Andy Scott
Fahredin Sheho   Alok Kumar Ray

The Horn of Africa

Ethiopia        Djibouti

Somalia         Eritrea

The Poetry Posse 2019

Gail Weston Shazor * Albert Carrasco * Hülya N. Yılmaz
Jackie Davis Allen * Caroline Nazareno * Eliza Segiet
Alicja Maria Kuberska * Teresa E. Gallion * Joe Paire
Kimberly Burnham * Shareef Abdur – Rasheed
Ashok K. Bhargava * Elizabeth Castillo * Swapna Behera
Tezmin Ition Tsai * William S. Peters, Sr.

The Year of the Poet VI
August 2019

Featured Poets
Shola Balogun * Bharati Nayak
Monalisa Dash Dwibedy * Mbizo  Chirasha

Coexist

Southwest Asia

The Poetry Posse 2019

Gail Weston Shazor * Albert Carrasco * Hülya N. Yılmaz
Jackie Davis Allen * Caroline Nazareno * Eliza Segiet
Alicja Maria Kuberska * Teresa E. Gallion * Joe Paire
Kimberly Burnham * Shareef Abdur – Rasheed
Ashok K. Bhargava * Elizabeth Castillo * Swapna Behera
Tezmin Ition Tsai * William S. Peters, Sr.

Now Available

www.innerchildpress.com/the-year-of-the-poet

## The Year of the Poet VI
### September 2019

Featured Poets

Elena Liliana Popescu * Gobinda Biswas
Iram Fatima 'Ashi' * Joseph S. Spence, Sr.

### The Caucasus
The Poetry Posse 2019

Gail Weston Shazor * Albert Carasco * Hülya N. Yılmaz
Jackie Davis Allen * Caroline Nazareno * Eliza Segiet
Alicja Maria Kuberska * Teresa E. Gallion * Joe Paire
Kimberly Burnham * Shareef Abdur – Rasheed
Ashok K. Bhargava * Elizabeth Castillo * Swapna Behera
Tzemin Ition Tsai * William S. Peters, Sr.

## The Year of the Poet VI
### October 2019

Featured Poets

Ngozi Olivia Osuoha * Denisa Kondić
Pankhuri Sinha * Christena AV Williams

### The Nile Valley
The Poetry Posse 2019

Gail Weston Shazor * Albert Carasco * Hülya N. Yılmaz
Jackie Davis Allen * Caroline Nazareno * Eliza Segiet
Alicja Maria Kuberska * Teresa E. Gallion * Joe Paire
Kimberly Burnham * Shareef Abdur – Rasheed
Ashok K. Bhargava * Elizabeth Castillo * Swapna Behera
Tzemin Ition Tsai * William S. Peters, Sr.

## The Year of the Poet VI
### November 2019

Featured Poets

Rozalia Aleksandrova * Orbindu Ganga
Smruti Ranjan Mohanty * Sofia Skleida

### Northern Asia
The Poetry Posse 2019

Gail Weston Shazor * Albert Carasco * Hülya N. Yılmaz
Jackie Davis Allen * Caroline Nazareno * Eliza Segiet
Alicja Maria Kuberska * Teresa E. Gallion * Joe Paire
Kimberly Burnham * Shareef Abdur – Rasheed
Ashok K. Bhargava * Elizabeth Castillo * Swapna Behera
Tzemin Ition Tsai * William S. Peters, Sr.

## The Year of the Poet VI
### December 2019

Featured Poets

Rittika Kenani (Rittwika) * Sujana Paul
Bhawani Shanker * Kapardeli Eftichia

### Oceania
The Poetry Posse 2019

Gail Weston Shazor * Albert Carasco * Hülya N. Yılmaz
Jackie Davis Allen * Caroline Nazareno * Eliza Segiet
Alicja Maria Kuberska * Teresa E. Gallion * Joe Paire
Kimberly Burnham * Shareef Abdur – Rasheed
Ashok K. Bhargava * Elizabeth Castillo * Swapna Behera
Tzemin Ition Tsai * William S. Peters, Sr.

## Now Available

www.innerchildpress.com/the-year-of-the-poet

## The Year of the Poet VII
### January 2020

**Featured Poets**

B S Tyagi * Ashok Chakravarthy Tholana
Andy Scott * Anwer Ghani

1901 Jean Henry Dunant and Frédéric Passy

The Year of Peace
Celebrating past Nobel Peace Prize Recipients

### The Poetry Posse 2020

Gail Weston Shazor * Albert Carasco * Hülya N. Yılmaz
Jackie Davis Allen * Caroline Nazareno * Eliza Segiet
Alicja Maria Kuberska * Teresa E. Gallion * Joe Paire
Kimberly Burnham * Shareef Abdur – Rasheed
Ashok K. Bhargava * Elizabeth Castillo * Swapna Behera
Tezmin Ition Tsai * William S. Peters, Sr.

## The Year of the Poet VII
### February 2020

**Featured Poets**

Jennifer Ades * Martina Reisz Newberry
Ibrahim Honjo * Claudia Piccinno

Henri La Fontaine ~ 1913

The Year of Peace
Celebrating past Nobel Peace Prize Recipients

### The Poetry Posse 2020

Gail Weston Shazor * Albert Carasco * Hülya N. Yılmaz
Jackie Davis Allen * Caroline Nazareno * Eliza Segiet
Alicja Maria Kuberska * Teresa E. Gallion * Joe Paire
Kimberly Burnham * Shareef Abdur – Rasheed
Ashok K. Bhargava * Elizabeth Castillo * Swapna Behera
Tezmin Ition Tsai * William S. Peters, Sr.

## The Year of the Poet VII
### March 2020

**Featured Poets**

Aziz Mountassir * Krishna Paraisa
Hannie Rouweler * Rozalia Aleksandrova

Aristide Briand ~ 1926 ~ Gustav Stresemann

The Year of Peace
Celebrating past Nobel Peace Prize Recipients

### The Poetry Posse 2020

Gail Weston Shazor * Albert Carasco * Hülya N. Yılmaz
Jackie Davis Allen * Caroline Nazareno * Eliza Segiet
Alicja Maria Kuberska * Teresa E. Gallion * Joe Paire
Kimberly Burnham * Shareef Abdur – Rasheed
Ashok K. Bhargava * Elizabeth Castillo * Swapna Behera
Tezmin Ition Tsai * William S. Peters, Sr.

## The Year of the Poet VII
### April 2020

**Featured Poets**

Rohini Behera * Mircea Dan Duta
Monalisa Dash Dwibedy * NilavroNill Shoovro

Carlos Saavedra Lamas ~ 1936

The Year of Peace
Celebrating past Nobel Peace Prize Recipients

### The Poetry Posse 2020

Gail Weston Shazor * Albert Carasco * Hülya N. Yılmaz
Jackie Davis Allen * Caroline Nazareno * Eliza Segiet
Alicja Maria Kuberska * Teresa E. Gallion * Joe Paire
Kimberly Burnham * Shareef Abdur – Rasheed
Ashok K. Bhargava * Elizabeth Castillo * Swapna Behera
Tezmin Ition Tsai * William S. Peters, Sr.

*Now Available*

www.innerchildpress.com/the-year-of-the-poet

## The Year of the Poet VII
### May 2020

#### Featured Poets
Alok Kumar Ray * Eden S. Trinidad
Franco Barbato * Izabela Zubko

### Ralph Bunche ~ 1950

The Year of Peace
Celebrating past Nobel Peace Prize Recipients

#### The Poetry Posse 2020
Gail Weston Shazor * Albert Carasco * Hülya N. Yılmaz
Jackie Davis Allen * Caroline Nazareno * Eliza Segiet
Alicja Maria Kuberska * Teresa E. Gallion * Joe Paire
Kimberly Burnham * Shareef Abdur – Rasheed
Ashok K. Bhargava * Elizabeth Castillo * Swapna Behera
Tezmin Ition Tsai * William S. Peters, Sr.

## The Year of the Poet VII
### June 2020

#### Featured Poets
Eftichia Kapardeli * Metin Cengiz
Hussein Habasch * Kosh K Mathew

### Albert John Lutuli ~ 1960

The Year of Peace
Celebrating past Nobel Peace Prize Recipients

#### The Poetry Posse 2020
Gail Weston Shazor * Albert Carasco * Hülya N. Yılmaz
Jackie Davis Allen * Caroline Nazareno * Eliza Segiet
Alicja Maria Kuberska * Teresa E. Gallion * Joe Paire
Kimberly Burnham * Shareef Abdur – Rasheed
Ashok K. Bhargava * Elizabeth Castillo * Swapna Behera
Tezmin Ition Tsai * William S. Peters, Sr.

## The Year of the Poet VII
### July 2020

#### Featured Poets
Mykola Martyniuk * Orbindu Ganga
Roula Pollard * Kam Praktisha

### Norman Ernest Borlaug ~ 1970

The Year of Peace
Celebrating past Nobel Peace Prize Recipients

#### The Poetry Posse 2020
Gail Weston Shazor * Albert Carasco * Hülya N. Yılmaz
Jackie Davis Allen * Caroline Nazareno * Eliza Segiet
Alicja Maria Kuberska * Teresa E. Gallion * Joe Paire
Kimberly Burnham * Shareef Abdur – Rasheed
Ashok K. Bhargava * Elizabeth Castillo * Swapna Behera
Tezmin Ition Tsai * William S. Peters, Sr.

## The Year of the Poet VII
### August 2020

#### Featured Poets
Dr Pragya Suman * Chinh Nguyen
Srinivas Vasudev * Ugwu Leonard Ifeanyi, Jr.

### Adolfo Pérez Esquivel ~ 1980

The Year of Peace
Celebrating past Nobel Peace Prize Recipients

#### The Poetry Posse 2020
Gail Weston Shazor * Albert Carasco * Hülya N. Yılmaz
Jackie Davis Allen * Caroline Nazareno * Eliza Segiet
Alicja Maria Kuberska * Teresa E. Gallion * Joe Paire
Kimberly Burnham * Shareef Abdur – Rasheed
Ashok K. Bhargava * Elizabeth Castillo * Swapna Behera
Tezmin Ition Tsai * William S. Peters, Sr.

## Now Available

www.innerchildpress.com/the-year-of-the-poet

## The Year of the Poet VII
### September 2020

#### Featured Poets
Racil Anu Al-Jishi • Indlovovic Sindane
Dr. Brijesh Kumar Gupta • Urmil Najjar

**Mikhail Sergeyevich Gorbachev ~ 1990**

The Year of Peace
Celebrating past Nobel Peace Prize Recipients

### The Poetry Posse 2020
Gail Weston Shazor • Albert Carasco • Hülya N. Yılmaz
Jackie Davis Allen • Caroline Nazareno • Eliza Segiet
Alicja Maria Kuberska • Teresa E. Gallion • Joe Paire
Kimberly Burnham • Shareef Abdur – Rasheed
Ashok K. Bhargava • Elizabeth Castillo • Swapna Behera
Tezmin Ition Tsai • William S. Peters, Sr.

## The Year of the Poet VII
### October 2020

#### Featured Poets
Mutawaf A. Shaheed • Galina Italyanskaya
Nadeem Fraz • Avril Tanya Meallem

**Kim Dae-jung ~ 2000**

The Year of Peace
Celebrating past Nobel Peace Prize Recipients

### The Poetry Posse 2020
Gail Weston Shazor • Albert Carasco • Hülya N. Yılmaz
Jackie Davis Allen • Caroline Nazareno • Eliza Segiet
Alicja Maria Kuberska • Teresa E. Gallion • Joe Paire
Kimberly Burnham • Shareef Abdur – Rasheed
Ashok K. Bhargava • Elizabeth Castillo • Swapna Behera
Tezmin Ition Tsai • William S. Peters, Sr.

## The Year of the Poet VII
### November 2020

#### Featured Poets
Elisa Mascia • Sue Lindenberg McClelland
Hatif Janabi • Jean Gaćina

**Liu Xiaobo ~ 2010**

The Year of Peace
Celebrating past Nobel Peace Prize Recipients

### The Poetry Posse 2020
Gail Weston Shazor • Albert Carasco • Hülya N. Yılmaz
Jackie Davis Allen • Caroline Nazareno • Eliza Segiet
Alicja Maria Kuberska • Teresa E. Gallion • Joe Paire
Kimberly Burnham • Shareef Abdur – Rasheed
Ashok K. Bhargava • Elizabeth Castillo • Swapna Behera
Tezmin Ition Tsai • William S. Peters, Sr.

## The Year of the Poet VII
### December 2020

#### Featured Poets
Ratan Ghosh • Ibtisam Ibrahim Al-Asady
Brindha Vinodh • Selma Kopic

**Abiy Ahmed Ali ~ 2019**

The Year of Peace
Celebrating past Nobel Peace Prize Recipients

### The Poetry Posse 2020
Gail Weston Shazor • Albert Carasco • Hülya N. Yılmaz
Jackie Davis Allen • Caroline Nazareno • Eliza Segiet
Alicja Maria Kuberska • Teresa E. Gallion • Joe Paire
Kimberly Burnham • Shareef Abdur – Rasheed
Ashok K. Bhargava • Elizabeth Castillo • Swapna Behera
Tezmin Ition Tsai • William S. Peters, Sr.

## Now Available

www.innerchildpress.com/the-year-of-the-poet

and there is much, much more !

visit . . .

www.innerchildpress.com/antho
logies-sales-special.php

Also check out our Authors and
all the wonderful Books
Available at :

www.innerchildpress.com/autho
rs-pages

# World Healing World Peace
## 2020

Poets for Humanity

*Now Available*

www.worldhealingworldpeacepoetry.com

INNER CHILD PRESS

# WORLD HEALING WORLD PEACE
## 2018

A Poetry Anthology for Humanity

*Now Available*

www.worldhealingworldpeacepoetry.com

i support

World Healing
World Peace

www.worldhealingworldpeacepoetry.com

World Healing
World Peace
2012, 2014, 2016, 2018, 2020

*Now Available*

www.worldhealingworldpeacepoetry.com

# Inner Child Press International

*'building bridges of cultural understanding'*

## Meet the Board of Directors

William S. Peters, Sr.
Chair Person
Founder
Inner Child Enterprises
Inner Child Press

Hülya N Yılmaz
Director
Editing Services
Co-Chair Person

Fahredin B. Shehu
Director
Cultural Affairs

Elizabeth E. Castillo
Director
Recording Secretary

De'Andre Hawthorne
Director
Performance Poetry

Gail Weston Shazor
Director
Anthologies

Kimberly Burnham
Director
Cultural Ambassador
Pacific Northwest
USA

Ashok K. Bhargava
Director
WIN Awards

Deborah Smart
Director
Publicity
Marketing

www.innerchildpress.com

# Inner Child Press International

*'building bridges of cultural understanding'*

## Meet our Cultural Ambassadors

**Fahredin Shehu**
Director of Cultural

**Faleha Hassan**
Iraq ~ USA

**Elizabeth E. Castillo**
Philippines

**Antoinette Coleman**
Chicago
Midwest USA

**Ananda Nepali**
Nepal ~ Tibet
Southern India

**Kimberly Burnham**
Pacific Northwest
USA

**Alicja Kuberska**
Poland
Eastern Europe

**Swapna Behera**
India
Southeast Asia

**Kolade O. Freedom**
Nigeria
West Africa

**Monsif Beroual**
Morocco
Northern Africa

**Ashok K. Bhargava**
Canada

**Tzemin Ition Tsai**
Republic of China
Greater China

**Alicia M. Ramirez**
Mexico
Central America

**Christena AV Williams**
Jamaica
Caribbean

**Louise Hudon**
Eastern Canada

**Aziz Mountassir**
Morocco
Northern Africa

**Shareef Abdur-Rasheed**
Southeastern USA

**Laure Charazac**
France
Western Europe

**Mohammad Ikbal Harb**
Lebanon
Middle East

**Mohamed Abdel
Aziz Shmeis**
Egypt
Middle East

**Hilary Mainga**
Kenya
Eastern Africa

**Josephus R. Johnson**
Liberia

## www.innerchildpress.com

This Anthological Publication
is underwritten solely by

*Inner Child Press International*

Inner Child Press is a Publishing Company
Founded and Operated by Writers. Our
personal publishing experiences provides
us an intimate understanding of the
sometimes daunting challenges Writers,
New and Seasoned may face in the
Business of Publishing and Marketing
their Creative "Written Work".

For more Information

*Inner Child Press International*

www.innerchildpress.com

Inner Child Press International

'building bridges of cultural understanding'     www.innerchildpress.com
202 Wiltree Court, State College, Pennsylvania 16801

~ fini ~

www.ingramcontent.com/pod-product-compliance
Lightning Source LLC
LaVergne TN
LVHW051045080426
835508LV00019B/1705